I've known Ron for decades, and I've never had a conversation with him that wasn't punctuated with laughter, thoughtfulness, and honesty. More than that, though, the conversations always lead to Jesus. Ron's faith is integrated into every corner of his life, from his family to the books he loves to the way he plays guitar solos. *Abiding Dependence* reads like one of those great after-show conversations with Ron, which go from banjo practice to Scripture, from George MacDonald to fatherhood, from Narnia to The Lord of the Rings—and where I walk away resting in the truth that Jesus loves me.

ANDREW PETERSON
Singer-songwriter; author of *The God of the Garden* and *The Wingfeather Saga*

Every conversation I've ever had with Ron Block has left me more encouraged, hopeful, and aware of Jesus' kindness toward me. I'm so thankful for this book. *Abiding Dependence* lets me start each morning with this wise and thoughtful friend, and helps me better begin each day in the safe and generous embrace of Jesus.

ANDREW OSENGA
Singer-songwriter; *The Pivot* podcast; Director of A&R at Integrity Music

Ron Block's profound talent, combined with an acute and dogged determination to get things musically perfect, have made him one of the greatest living banjo players on the planet. It's a marvel to see that same determination come to play in his desire to know, follow, and abide in God as expressed in the tender and poignant devotions collected here. This is a book that one can turn to again and again for guidance in seeking God on a daily basis.

FERNANDO ORTEGA
Singer, composer, and photographer

For nearly twenty years I've been the recipient of Ron's treasure chest of biblical insight. You too can discover spiritual riches and transformative truth in *Abiding Dependence*. Dive in deep and behold the gems!

STEVE BERGER
Ambassador Services International

What a joy . . . I have known Ron for over twenty-five years, and his art, heart, and friendship have enriched my life tremendously. Ron understands as well as anybody I know that the gospel puts an end to all performing and merit. Jesus has done for us, and does in us, what we could never do for ourselves. Our union with Jesus, and communion with Him, is the sum and substance of the

Christian life. There is only one love better than life, and it is His for us. Thank you, my brother and friend.

SCOTTY SMITH
Pastor Emeritus, Christ Community Church; Teacher in Residence, West End Community Church

If you buy only one devotional book, this needs to be it. While many books tell you what to do, this one tells you who you are and who He is in such a way that you'll find yourself responding to grace in a way that will truly transform you.

STEVE MCVEY
Bestselling author, *Grace Walk*

There are two words that are synonymous with Ron Block: clarity and tone. His heart and head are filled with both, so it's not surprising they come out of his mouth and hands. He's been widely recognized for the clarity and tone he produces musically, now people have the opportunity to discover the source of his abilities. This book presents clear, practical, understandable truth as to what life with Jesus can be like. You'll find yourself inspired and empowered by the rich tones of grace that will lift you into peace, joy, and fulfillment—all precious commodities in our current culture.

KENNY THACKER
Founder, SoundWord, Inc

Ron Block has blessed us by inviting us into his inner thoughts and communion with God. His confidence in the Father's unconditional love expresses itself in an inviting freedom.

DUDLEY HALL
Kerygma Ventures; author of *Grace Works*

Amidst all the clatter and chaos of our current age, I urge you to invite these words deep into the activity of your soul's posture. I think you'll discover much of what you've been aching to find.

REBECCA K. REYNOLDS
Author of *Courage, Dear Heart: Letters to a Weary World*

Abiding Dependence by Ron Block is not only a great devotional, it is a must-read for anyone wishing to come to know their true identity in Christ and the power they experience as they walk in that relationship. Realizing you are loved unconditionally by the Father causes one to experience the peace that passes all understanding. Again, this book is a must-read.

CRAIG SNYDER
Executive Director of Grace Walk Ministries

Living

Moment

ABIDING DEPENDENCE

by

Moment

in the Love of God

Ron Block

MOODY PUBLISHERS
CHICAGO

© 2022 by
RON BLOCK

All rights reserved. No part of this book may be reproduced in any form without permission in writing from the publisher, except in the case of brief quotations embodied in critical articles or reviews.

All Scripture quotations, unless otherwise indicated, are taken from the New King James Version. Copyright © 1982 by Thomas Nelson. Used by permission. All rights reserved.

Scripture quotations marked ESV are from the *ESV® Bible* (*The Holy Bible, English Standard Version®*), Copyright © 2001 by Crossway, a publishing ministry of Good News Publishers. Used by permission. All rights reserved.

Scripture quotations marked KJV are taken from the King James Version.

Scripture quotations marked NET are from the NET Bible® copyright ©1996, 2019 by Biblical Studies Press, L.L.C. http://netbible.com All rights reserved.

Scripture quotations marked (NLT) are taken from the Holy Bible, New Living Translation, copyright ©1996, 2004, 2015 by Tyndale House Foundation. Used by permission of Tyndale House Publishers, a Division of Tyndale House Ministries, Carol Stream, Illinois 60188. All rights reserved.

Emphasis in Scripture has been added.

Edited by Mackenzie Conway
Cover and interior design: Erik M. Peterson
Cover illustration of tree copyright © 2020 by Alexandr Bakanov / Adobe Stock (220041078).
All rights reserved.
Cover illustration of person copyright © 2020 by Alexandr Bakanov / Adobe Stock (145846612).
All rights reserved.
Author photo credit: Tanner Morris Photography

Library of Congress Cataloging-in-Publication Data

Names: Block, Ron, 1964- author.
Title: Abiding dependence : living moment-by-moment in the love of God /
Ron Block.
Description: Chicago : Moody Publishers, [2022] | Includes bibliographical
references. | Summary: "Abiding Dependence shares forty days of
meditations-a deep plunge into the beauty and richness of the Gospels.
The reader learns to breathe in the atmosphere of God's abiding love.
Musician Ron Block gives Christians soul strengthening hope not just for
a future someday but for this day"-- Provided by publisher.
Identifiers: LCCN 2022015422 (print) | LCCN 2022015423 (ebook) | ISBN
9780802424747 (paperback) | ISBN 9780802476975 (ebook)
Subjects: LCSH: God (Christianity)--Love--Meditations. | Jesus
Christ--Person and offices--Meditations. | Spirituality
(Christianity)--Meditations. | BISAC: RELIGION / Christian Living /
Inspirational | RELIGION / Christian Ministry / Pastoral Resources
Classification: LCC BT140 .B56 2022 (print) | LCC BT140 (ebook) | DDC
231/.6--dc23/eng/20220613
LC record available at https://lccn.loc.gov/2022015422
LC ebook record available at https://lccn.loc.gov/2022015423

Originally delivered by fleets of horse-drawn wagons, the affordable paperbacks from D. L. Moody's publishing house resourced the church and served everyday people. Now, after more than 125 years of publishing and ministry, Moody Publishers' mission remains the same—even if our delivery systems have changed a bit. For more information on other books (and resources) created from a biblical perspective, go to www.moodypublishers.com or write to:

Moody Publishers
820 N. LaSalle Boulevard
Chicago, IL 60610

1 3 5 7 9 10 8 6 4 2

Printed in the United States of America

To my mother,
Joyce Marilyn Block.
You loved me with the love of Jesus,
And I saw His face reflected in your joy
When He came to take you Home.

Contents

Introduction

I've been playing music for over forty years, and I know as settled fact if my guitar is out of tune it won't matter how well I play. I could play the most beautifully expressive solo I've ever performed and it would still sound bad. My solo might be well-conceived in my mind, but the tuning would destroy anyone's experience of hearing it. My intention would be good, but since I didn't take the time to tune my instrument properly, my immediate future with the band would certainly be less than optimal.

Spending a little time recognizing God's presence tunes up our hearts and minds before the day begins. That's what I hope to offer in this book—encouragement toward fellowship with God. I'll say here at the beginning that I don't like the phrase "devotional time." It smacks of "doing time" and obligation rather than delight. But time with God is not a "rule" we have to keep. We can opt out, avoid it, do things our own way, live from our false identities, and try to get love and identity from every other place but in God our Father, our Abba. God gives us the choice, and "there is therefore now no condemnation to those who are in Christ Jesus" (Rom. 8:1).

But if we do choose to rush out on stage without tuning up, we also reap the consequences—not punishment, just natural consequences. If I don't tune my guitar, if I don't pay attention to my car's gas gauge, if I don't eat healthy food, there are natural consequences that result. No one is punishing me; I am punishing myself, making my life less than it could be.

The Father invites us to His easy chair, invites us to come sit with Him. And there, as we pour our thoughts and feelings out to Him, become silent, and rest in His presence, He will begin to teach us the ways, the responsibilities, the privileges, the rights, and more centrally, the identity and continual union we have in Him as His sons and daughters. He will tell us who we are, who we aren't, and He will want us to say it back to Him, like a child reciting lessons. He will show us promises in His written Word, and will want to hear us read them back, aloud, to make that written Word stir up the living Word inside us, to make that Word become the central hub in how we see Him, life, ourselves, and others.

> *The Father invites us to His easy chair, invites us to come sit with Him. And there, He will begin to teach us the ways, the responsibilities, the privileges, the rights, and more centrally, the identity and continual union we have in Him as His sons and daughters.*

I'm not saying we'll always *feel* better after this set-aside time, or that ten minutes later we won't forget who we are. But over time, this resting in God, fellowshiping with God, knowing Him—this closeness of relationship begins to produce an inner, settled *confidence* as we go about our daily life.

We don't do this to get God to come down from heaven to us; He's already in us, around us, and everywhere. It's not something we do to get God to love us or like us; He already loves us beyond any earthly love. We don't do it to become more spiritual, because every one of us has been given the same Spirit.

We do it for the same reason a four-year-old daughter comes out in the morning and sits sleepy-eyed and close with her dad on the couch, or a young son asks if his dad wants to sit and play LEGOs with him. We do it as a child asks their mom about a problem at school or a man asks an older, wiser friend and mentor about a relationship issue. God is all these things to us, and infinitely more.

None of this is an obligation. Rather, we can play in the mud outside, try to get others to like and value us, be "good" Christians by our self-effort. But little of it will matter in the end; what will matter is that we sat in the easy chair with Abba, our Father, learning our lessons, learning His promises, learning our identity in Him, and recognizing our union with Him. What will matter is that we stepped out into the wide world to live through His life-giving Spirit.

We can get to know God not solely by reading the Bible or books written *about* Him, but by recognizing Him as real and as present as a close friend sitting and having coffee with us. Except He's even closer, because God, in Christ, by the Holy Spirit, is *inside* you. He knows how you think, what you think you want, and what you truly want and need. He knows your history, your problems, and everything people have said or done to you. He knows every detail of everything you've ever said or done, and yet He loves you with His river of wholehearted commitment-love.

He wants us to spend time with Him so that you and I become our real selves and find Him as our source, our center, shucking off all the false identities, masks, and shields we've donned to deal with life in this world.

And if a God like that sounds weird to you, well, you may have been sold oceanfront property in Death Valley.

Day 1

Life and Breath

And the LORD God formed man of the dust of the ground,
and breathed into his nostrils the breath of life; and man
became a living being.

GENESIS 2:7

And so it is written, "The first man Adam became a living
being." The last Adam became a life-giving spirit.

1 CORINTHIANS 15:45

I know you've only just started reading, but stop and breathe in deeply for a moment.

I know. I've read books that tell me to do things, like "Breathe" or "Write down any thoughts you have right now," and I wouldn't do it. I'd skip and skim through things like that because I was interested only in *information*, sincerely believing more information would produce transformation. Alas, it didn't.

So, amuse me. Take a big, deep breath for four seconds, from your diaphragm. Hold it for four seconds. Breathe out for four seconds. Do it again. Feel your body relax? It feels good.

We need oxygen—big, deep breaths of fresh air—to *thrive.* Breath keeps our bodies alive. We can go without food for weeks and without water for days—without breath, only a few minutes.

Just as we need breath to fuel our bodies, our humanity is meant to be powered by the Breath of God—the Holy Spirit, the *pneuma.*[1]

The apostle John says, "God is love" (1 John 4:8). John doesn't say God *has* love and gives love to us as a *thing,* but that He *is* love. His very Being—the Holy Spirit—*is* love. The Holy Spirit is the breath of love in your heart, your soul, your spirit, your mind. When we're getting low on love, we need to take a moment to fill up the tank. "Be filled with the Spirit," says the apostle Paul (Eph. 5:18).

As believers, we need to learn to breathe in deeply this Holy Breath of the Person of God: God our Love, God our Life.

C. S. Lewis wrote in *Mere Christianity,*

> The real problem of the Christian life comes where people do not usually look for it. It comes the very moment you wake up each morning. All your wishes and hopes for the day rush at you like wild animals. And the first job each morning consists simply in shoving them all back; in listening to that other voice, taking that other point of view, letting that other larger, stronger, quieter life come flowing in. And so on, all day. Standing back from all your natural fussings and frettings; coming in out of the wind.
>
> We can only do it for moments at first. But from those moments the new sort of life will be spreading through our system.[2]

We don't usually look for this because we're so geared to the mindset of *doing.* We spring out of bed and *do, do, do,* stuffing down feelings of anxiety, stress, insufficiency, or even worthlessness with coffee and an egg on toast. But without spending moments of time simply *being* with God, without receiving that infusion of the Holy Spirit, we wither and become increasingly subject to fear and anxiety; we listen to any and every voice but our Father's. If we want to live above this low level of life, we'd be wise to follow George MacDonald's advice:

> But he who would be born again indeed,
> Must wake his soul unnumbered times a day . . .
> Submiss and ready to the making will,
> Athirst and empty, for God's breath to fill.[3]

If we begin to make a habit throughout the day of taking a moment for the Breath of God, to recognize His reality and presence, we'll see a deepening spiritual vitality.

In my years playing with Alison Krauss & Union Station, I've had times when I was down on my playing. Before a show I'd have a feeling of anxiety—worries about making mistakes. This anxious attitude often led to me making *more* mistakes, and it began to put tension into my arms and hands.

I began going into a dressing room before each show, closing my eyes, breathing in and out deeply, and recognizing the Lord as present with me and in me, thanking Him for the work He's done in me and through our music.

Without spending moments of time simply being with God, without receiving that infusion of the Holy Spirit, we wither and become increasingly subject to fear and anxiety; we listen to any and every voice but our Father's.

Over a few days of this, I became less and less anxious, and when showtime came, I began to step out on stage with more confidence, joy, and expectation of a great show—and I played better.

Anxiety and fear eat up our "processing power" and get us self-focused. Living life well requires presence, and we can't have presence if we're walking in self-conscious fear. Taking brief moments to breathe and rest in the awareness of God's presence makes a big difference in our courage and ability to face the day.

Day 2

Jesus, the Son of God

If there be a God, he must hear you if you call to him. If there be a father, he will listen to his child. He will teach you everything.... Read the story of our Saviour as if you had never read it before. He at least was a man who seemed to have that secret of life after the knowledge of which your heart is longing.

GEORGE MACDONALD

That secret of life": our hearts long to know it, not just our heads.

When I was in my late teens and early twenties, my pastor would say, "Most people don't put flesh and blood on the Bible." He meant that many of us read the Bible not really imagining what it was like to be there taking part as a human being. We don't give much thought to what Moses, Caleb, Isaiah, Jesus, or others felt or thought as they lived out those stories.

The story of Jesus in the Gospels, when we read it as if for the first time, reveals His secret of life.

Jesus Himself is the way, the truth, and the life; the beginning and the end; the author and finisher of faith.[1] If we want to know what a stronger, deeper, better, more joyful Holy Spirit–filled life can be for us, Jesus is the center of it.

Jesus is the culmination of thousands of years of promises from God coming down to a single point in history when God Himself was born into a human body, *God with us* (Matt. 1:23). If we want to know how to walk in the ways of God, to live and speak the truth of God, and to live filled with the life of God, the best place to begin is with the God-Man, who said, "I am the way, the truth, and the life. No one comes to the Father except through Me" (John 14:6).

The Gospels can help us put flesh and blood on Jesus, the disciples, and all the people interacting with them, rather than seeing the Bible as a collection of doctrinal concepts. We all have our perspectives, expectations, and experiences, and often read the Bible with something like a veil over our eyes. If it's a passage or book we've already studied, we think we *know* it, and so we learn little.

The Bible is a many-layered document that continues to deepen as we grow. We don't worship the Bible; its job is to point us to Jesus, to God, to the Holy Spirit, so that we worship God in spirit and in truth.

When we open our minds and hearts, praying for wisdom before reading, we're asking to *learn*. It's childlike and humble.

When we read the Gospels, setting aside what we *think* we know, we see a Jesus who is always loving but honest, kind though strong, compassionate but not letting people off the hook, wise yet continually asking questions. The God we see in

Jesus in the Gospels is not what many think of as a "religious person"—someone austere, stoic, and often disapproving. If you wanted to start an elitist religion, you sure wouldn't start with Jesus, because He was often saying things to religious people that lit their hair on fire.

In the Gospels, we see Him associate with every level of society, rich and poor, religious leaders, thieves, prostitutes, fishermen, soldiers, and other races; He doesn't seem to recognize social divisions between people. He goes into the temple and into synagogues. He attends parties, feasts, and weddings, is branded as a glutton and a drunkard, walks willingly among lepers, blind beggars, loose women, and demon-possessed people, and is accused continually of breaking religious laws.

When we read the Gospels, setting aside what we think we know, we see a Jesus who is always loving but honest, kind though strong, compassionate but not letting people off the hook, wise yet continually asking questions.

Dorothy Sayers wrote, "What does the Church think of Christ? The Church's answer is categorical and uncompromising, and it is this: that Jesus Bar-Joseph, the carpenter of Nazareth, was in fact and in truth, and in the most exact and literal sense of the words, the God 'by whom all things were made.'"[2]

"The Word became flesh and dwelt among us" (John 1:14).

In the Gospels, through Jesus, we begin to see what God is truly like. Jesus said to Philip, "He who has seen Me has seen the Father; so how can you say, 'Show us the Father'?" (John 14:9). Jesus is the declaration of God, the unfolding of God's nature to us. If we want to know God's thoughts, attitudes, and actions, we can read about Jesus in the Gospels with an open, childlike mind, ready to hear, ready to see. "No one has seen God at any time. The only begotten Son, who is in the bosom of the Father, He has declared Him" (John 1:18).

Day 3

Jesus, the Son of Man

> Have this mind among yourselves, which is yours in
> Christ Jesus, who, though he was in the form of God, did
> not count equality with God a thing to be grasped, but
> emptied himself, by taking the form of a servant, being
> born in the likeness of men. And being found in human
> form, he humbled himself by becoming obedient to the
> point of death, even death on a cross.
>
> PHILIPPIANS 2:5–8 ESV

I grew up thinking of Jesus mostly as God in human form, believing when He lived as a man on earth, He lived and acted as the second person of the Trinity. Now, of course Jesus was and *is* God in human form. But when I was a boy and young man, the idea that Jesus in the Gospels lived His earthly life as an infinitely powerful, all-knowing being put a vast, unbridgeable gulf between His life and character and any love, compassion, kindness, or strength I could ever develop.

But Philippians tells us Jesus emptied Himself to become fully human, to be just like you and me—that is, to be *a servant*. A servant's job is to obey, to take care of the needs of another person. It isn't that Jesus ceased to be the eternal Son of God, or lost His place in the Trinity, or emptied Himself of deity, but as we will see, He set aside the *use* of His *own* authority, power, and knowledge; the unlimited God limited Himself to fully identify with our humanness—to live as we are meant to live, listening and obeying the Holy Spirit. Jesus Christ often called Himself "the Son of Man."

> *Jesus emptied Himself to become fully human, to be just like you and me—that is, to be* a servant.

If you were a rich, powerful Christian on a mission trip, you wouldn't pull up to the village in a Lamborghini, step out in a Brioni suit, and throw around wads of cash. You'd leave your car, suit, and power behind, give money to the missions organization, and put yourself under their orders. You'd wear ordinary clothes and be willing to get your hands dirty. You'd still be important in the eyes of your people back home, but you'd sacrifice appearances and the use of your power for love's sake, humbling yourself to help others.

This is how Jesus can be 100 percent God yet 100 percent man. Even though Jesus was God and remained God, He set aside the use of His privileges as God. Otherwise, we couldn't say Jesus was 100 percent human, because God is present everywhere, knows everything, and is all-powerful, while humans are not.

To understand the infinite God, to really *see* what He is like, we had to see Him in our human clothes. *God humbled Himself for us because He loves us that much.*

God came to us as a helpless baby, formed in the belly of an unwed teenage girl. Doubtless, as God, He could have chosen to begin walking, talking, and doing miracles as a newborn. He didn't, because one of the reasons He came was to be kin with us, to be made one of us. To be human means to be *localized*, to *learn*, and be *limited*. This is how Jesus Christ, fully God, emptied Himself to be fully human.

Let's think on that for a few moments. God is omnipresent—that is, He's always present everywhere—but Jesus became *localized* in a single body. Among stable litter, sheep, and straw, amid rumors of scandal, He was born tiny and wet from Mary's body, in Bethlehem, with His father Joseph, to eventually grow up in the poor town of Nazareth.

God the Father is omniscient, but Jesus (in His humanity) had to *learn*: "Though He was a Son, yet He learned obedience by the things which He suffered" (Heb. 5:8). To learn is to grow and expand. As a toddler, He learned to talk and walk. As a boy, He learned all the jobs and tasks any ordinary boy had to learn growing up in the Middle East two thousand years ago. The apostle Luke writes, "And Jesus increased in wisdom and stature, and in favor with God and men" (Luke 2:52). If you are omniscient, you already know everything, but Jesus grew in wisdom like He grew in height.

The difficulties of the situations Jesus went through in the Gospels increased with the narrative, and His reliance and obedience rose to each challenge, culminating in His obedience even to death on the cross.

In the Gospels we see Jesus learn, because He sometimes *marveled*. The Greek word *thaumazō* translated "marveled" means a thing happened that people didn't foresee,[1] prompting surprise and wonder. To marvel is our human response to the unexpected. It's *astonishment*. There are various examples of people marveling in the Gospels, including Jesus.[2]

When Jesus was in Capernaum, a Roman centurion with a paralyzed, tormented servant walked up to Him and asked for healing. Jesus was about to go with him, but the centurion said, "Lord, I am not worthy that You should come under my roof. But only speak a word, and my servant will be healed. For I also am a man under authority, having soldiers under me. And I say to this one, 'Go,' and he goes; and to another, 'Come,' and he comes; and to my servant, 'Do this,' and he does it" (Matt. 8:8–9).

> *The difficulties of the situations Jesus went through in the Gospels increased with the narrative, and His reliance and obedience rose to each challenge, culminating in His obedience even to death on the cross.*

Jesus marveled in response, not expecting the level of trust and understanding displayed by this Roman. The centurion saw Jesus was under His Father's authority, that He had been given authority and power, and that He could use His delegated authority and power to get things done quickly and efficiently.

Jesus was so surprised and amazed He turned around to the Israelite crowd following Him and said, "Assuredly, I say to you, I have not found such great faith, not even in Israel!" (Matt. 8:10).

God is omnipotent—that is, He's all-powerful. The psalmist wrote of God, "Behold, He who keeps Israel shall neither slumber nor sleep" (Ps. 121:4). But Jesus put on *limitation*. In the Gospels, we see Him grow tired, needing sleep. Not only did He need sleep, but Jesus had to take time alone with His Father after long periods of teaching or ministry, needing to renew His spiritual, emotional, and physical strength. He became weak when He fasted. He thirsted and hungered just as we do.

Although He was God and remained God, Jesus became fully human and embraced limitation, becoming a servant, living as a man filled with and empowered by His Father. He brought the unlimited God into human form. Jesus Christ is the doorway for our finite minds to see, know, and comprehend who God is and what He is like so we can embrace God as our Father.

Day 4

Jesus, the Tempted Son of Man

Immediately the Spirit drove Him into the wilderness.
And He was there in the wilderness forty days, tempted
by Satan, and was with the wild beasts; and the angels
ministered to Him.

MARK 1:12-13

If Jesus lived His human life solely as God, He couldn't have been tempted (James 1:13). God cannot be tempted by evil, but Jesus "was in all points tempted as we are, yet without sin" (Heb. 4:15). "In *all* points tempted as we are." We often jump to the next bit, "yet without sin." But let's pause for a moment and look at perhaps the most crucial point in the humanity of Jesus—temptation. Since we often confuse our own temptations with sin, we don't believe He experienced real temptation. If we don't believe that He did, we won't see how much He understands us in ours.

James speaks of temptation as enticement. "But each one is tempted when he is drawn away by his own desires and enticed" (James 1:14). To be tempted, we must first want something. We desire many things—food, esteem, sex, a sense of well-being, importance, security, stability, comfort—and all of them are natural, God-created desires of our humanity. But temptation pulls on our natural desires, prompting us to fulfill them in wrong ways, using our own power.

Temptation pulls on our natural desires, prompting us to fulfill them in wrong ways, using our own power.

After Jesus had been fasting for forty days in the wilderness, the tempter began, "If You are the Son of God, command that these stones become bread" (Matt. 4:3). In a sense, he pressed, *Prove Your identity. Command a miracle to feed Your desire. Use Your own authority and power as the Son of God.*

Jesus was hungry—even starving. His desire for food wasn't wrong. But the tempter latched on to it, wanting Him to focus on His hunger and act *as God* by His own authority and power to make stones into bread. But as a human, Jesus was not speaking or acting on His own authority. He later told the disciples, "The words that I speak to you I do not speak on My own authority; but the Father who dwells in Me does the works" (John 14:10). Though fully God, He wouldn't compromise His mission of being fully human.

"Then the devil took Him up into the holy city, set Him on the pinnacle of the temple, and said to Him, 'If You are the Son of God, throw Yourself down. For it is written: "He shall give His angels charge over you," and, "In their hands they shall bear you up, lest you dash your foot against a stone"'" (Matt. 4:5–6). The tempter enticed, *Prove You are the Son of God to the world. Be spectacular. The angels will catch You and everyone will see it. You'll have lots of followers.*

Jesus wanted to be what God had called Him to be, and the tempter latched on to this good desire. He was tempting Jesus to prove Himself, to test God, and to speed up God's timetable for His ministry. The enemy twisted Scripture to add weight to the temptation.

"Again, the devil took Him up on an exceedingly high mountain, and showed Him all the kingdoms of the world and their glory. And he said to Him, 'All these things I will give You if You will fall down and worship me'" (Matt. 4:8–9). *Here's the easy way out, Jesus, with no suffering. I've got the keys to the world; I'll give them to You if You worship me.* Jesus was offered the world with no cross.

If Jesus were living and acting *as God*, and "God cannot be tempted by evil" (James 1:13), these temptations would have been a meaningless farce.

We all get hungry. We want others to think well of us. We want to have a sense of purpose and live fulfilling lives—hopefully without too much trouble or suffering. These are all *normal* human wants. Temptation pulls on our God-given, normal desires, gets our minds and hearts off God, and leads us to fulfill our wants in wrong, destructive ways. The tempter wants us to take the quicker, easier path by our own human power and usurped authority.

When I read the Bible accounts of people being tempted, from Eve and Adam to Sarai and Abram, to Moses, Samson, Saul, David, and on to Jesus, the essential component of temptation is *independence.* Temptation says, "God isn't enough. He's working too slowly. Rely on yourself. You can figure it out."

Jesus listened internally to His Father, trusting Him with the fulfillment of His desires in His Father's timing. Power to resist came as He relied on the Holy Spirit within Himself. As He listened to His Father, Scriptures also rose into His mind. He responded:

"It is written, 'Man shall not live by bread alone, but by every word that proceeds from the mouth of God'" (Matt. 4:4).

"Again it is written, 'You shall not put the Lord your God to the test'" (Matt. 4:7 ESV).

"Away with you, Satan! For it is written, 'You shall worship the LORD your God, and Him only you shall serve'" (Matt. 4:10).

Three years later, the night He was betrayed, Jesus knew He was eating His last Passover meal. At the supper, He "was troubled in spirit, and testified and said, 'Most assuredly, I say to you, one of you will betray Me'" (John 13:21). The word "troubled" is *tarassō*,[1] meaning agitated, disturbed, anxious, distressed, or disquieted. We can't skim over the fact that Jesus didn't always *feel* calm and composed. We see Him experience strong emotions in the Gospels. He wept and "groan[ed] within Himself" with indignation (John 11:35, 38). He got angry, was grieved, and felt compassion and pity (Mark 3:5; Matt. 9:36).

As Judas slipped out of the room, Jesus knew what would follow: desertion by His disciples, interrogation, beatings, torture, crucifixion, becoming sin for us, and ultimately His heart-bursting cry, "My God, My God, why have You forsaken Me?" (Matt. 27:46; Ps. 22:1).

He took the disciples to Gethsemane that night, and in Mark's account, we can see His humanity in full focus. "And He took Peter, James, and John with Him, and He began to be troubled and deeply distressed. Then He said to them, 'My soul is exceedingly sorrowful, even to death. Stay here and watch'" (Mark 14:33–34).

He went a little further, fell to the ground, and prayed three times, "O My Father, if it is possible, let this cup pass from Me; nevertheless, not as I will, but as You will" (Matt. 26:39).

Let's think on this. The Father, the Son, the Holy Spirit are all of one spirit, mind, and purpose. "Hear, O Israel: The LORD our God, the LORD is one!" (Deut. 6:4). There are no arguments, no separate wills in the Trinity. There is one will, one plan—one God.

But Jesus was living as a human, depending on the Father, and what healthy human *wants* suffering? He *didn't know* if there was another way, so He asked the Father three times. The temptation to find a way out was so powerful that Luke records, "And being in agony, He prayed more earnestly. Then His sweat became like great drops of blood falling down to the ground" (Luke 22:44). The book of Hebrews says,

> who, in the days of His flesh, when He had offered up prayers and supplications, with vehement cries and tears to Him who was able to save Him from death, and was heard because of His godly fear, though He was a Son, yet He learned obedience by the things which He suffered. (Heb. 5:7–8)

Because His emotions were so strong, Jesus was tempted to believe His will and His Father's weren't the same. The desires of His soul and body were magnified—the survival instinct, the natural desire to avoid suffering, the desire for simple pleasures like supper with His friends—but these weren't the deepest will in Him, the will of His Spirit.

Jesus raised these valid human desires and feelings to His Father and said, "Not as I will, but as You will" (Matt. 26:39). He laid them in His Father's hands, saying in effect, "My real will, my deepest will, is *Your* will." Jesus aligned His humanity—His emotions and natural human desires—with His Father's purpose and intention for His life.

He had fallen to the ground in agony, soaked with sweat. Now He stood up as King, the author and finisher of faith. In this last temptation to fulfill His purpose in a quicker, easier way, to want something other than the Father's will, He emerged victorious. His unity with the Father's will remained intact.

Jesus was tempted to a high level of intensity, but temptation isn't sin. He never gave in, because His connection with His Father never failed. "Therefore, in all things He had to be made like His brethren, that He might be a merciful and faithful High Priest in things pertaining to God, to make propitiation for the sins of the people. For in that He Himself has suffered, being tempted, He is able to aid those who are tempted" (Heb. 2:17–18).

Day 5

Jesus, Our Compassionate High Priest

For we do not have a High Priest who cannot sympathize
with our weaknesses, but was in all points tempted as we
are, yet without sin.

HEBREWS 4:15

Jesus was tempted not only in *some* ways, but in *all* ways as we
are—yet He didn't give in.

The heart of every temptation is to believe we're independent
selves, that we can figure out our own solutions and use our own
power to achieve them. In that moment, our eyes are pulled off
God's life in us. We're led to use our own thinking, desires, emotions, and intellect to get what we need by our own human will
and effort.

Every temptation is an appeal to let go of dependence on God's love for us, God's life and power in us, God's promises to us. A temptation is a pull to go the other way, to believe we're independent, as if we can see into eternity and know what is good and bad for us.

But are we ever independent? When Adam and Eve ate the fruit, they depended on the tempter's word. If Jesus had followed the enemy's advice, the enemy would then have controlled His thoughts, words, attitudes, and actions. If we choose "independence" and "my will," we're temporarily giving the reins of our hearts to our worst enemy.

Jesus is our compassionate High Priest because He understands all this from the inside. He experienced our deepest needs, our strongest emotions, and our full range of temptations.

A young boy often can't see why he is made to say "Please" and "Thank you," or why he is made to do dishes or clean up his room. He'd rather be free to do as he pleases because his present happiness is more important to him than his future good. He has no concept of how his present actions will affect his future. Good parents make him do what is best for his future self, as far as they know, because they want the best for him.

Giving in to temptation centers on the belief that God as our Father doesn't have our continual and eternal best interests at heart, that He doesn't understand us, that He's a petty, capricious tyrant who wants His own way and likes bossing us around. It involves the temporary suspension of our active trust in His continual presence and the Holy Spirit within us—the Holy Spirit who is there, able, ready, and willing to energize us with all the energy of God (Col. 1:29).

Jesus understands us and has compassion; He felt the tempter's pulls on His soul and body. He resisted by actively trusting and recognizing His Father as real, present, indwelling, powerful, and having His best interests at heart. By that restful reliance He embodied the proverb, "Trust in the LORD with all your heart, and lean not on your own understanding; in all your ways acknowledge Him, and He shall direct your paths" (Prov. 3:5–6).

In any situation, we make choices to believe either in the illusion of independence or in the reality of dependence. We choose to believe we are alone to "make our own way," or we walk in the truth that we are never alone with God in us, that Jesus is the way.

C. S. Lewis wrote about this illusion of independence in *Mere Christianity*:

Giving in to temptation involves the temporary suspension of our active trust in His continual presence and the Holy Spirit within us—the Holy Spirit who is there, able, ready, and willing to energize us with all the energy of God (Col. 1:29).

The more I resist Him and try to live on my own, the more I become dominated by my own heredity and upbringing and surroundings and natural desires. In fact, what I so proudly call "Myself" becomes merely the meeting place for trains of events which I never started and which I cannot stop. What I call "My wishes" become merely the desires thrown up by my physical organism or pumped into me by other men's thoughts or even suggested to me by devils. Eggs and alcohol and a good night's sleep will be the real origins of what I flatter myself by regarding as my own highly personal and discriminating decision to make love to the girl opposite to me in the railway carriage. Propaganda will be the real origin of what I regard as my own personal political ideas. I am not, in my natural state, nearly so much of a person as I like to believe: most of what I call "me" can be very easily explained. It is when I turn to Christ, when I give myself up to His Personality, that I first begin to have a real personality of my own.[1]

Young people with good parents will sometimes listen to the voices of anyone and everyone around them rather than the counsel of the two people in the world who love them most, want the best for them, and would even die for them. When they listen to other voices, are they following their own will, or the fears, agendas, grievances, and unbelief of others?

We *will* listen to and follow someone. Will I listen to the promptings and the counsel of God's life, wisdom, and strength in me?

We're to trust in our compassionate High Priest:

> "Abide in Me, and I in you. As the branch cannot bear fruit of itself, unless it abides in the vine, neither can you, unless you abide in Me.
>
> "I am the vine, you are the branches. He who abides in Me, and I in him, bears much fruit; for without Me you can do nothing." (John 15:4–5)

Jesus limited Himself to be like us, experiencing strong emotions, temptations, and every other negative and positive aspect of our humanity—yet without sin. He lived by the Holy Spirit. If we don't recognize Him as 100 percent human as well as being 100 percent God, we won't accept our own humanity; we won't see how our limitations and temptations are there to be filled up and empowered the same way. We'll equate our desires, feelings, and temptations with sin, and condemn ourselves for being weak and tempted. We'll miss His compassionate understanding for us, and we won't follow His lead.

Jesus is "the author and finisher of our faith" (Heb. 12:2) and the word for "author" there—*archēgos*—means chief leader, prince, captain, pioneer.[2] Jesus cuts the path through the mind- and heart-numbing jungle of religion, rules, and man's ideas that so quickly grows up around the throne of God, leading us into the presence of His Father and ours—Jesus, our compassionate High Priest.

Jesus cuts the path through the mind- and heart-numbing jungle of religion, rules, and man's ideas that so quickly grows up around the throne of God, leading us into the presence of His Father and ours— Jesus, our compassionate High Priest.

Dependence on His indwelling Father is the biggest identifying stamp of the earthly life of Jesus Christ. It's the root of His love, compassion, authority, and power. Independence, self-effort, and self-will found no home in Him; temptations couldn't win because Jesus knew the source and wellspring of life. He was battered by temptations, but He lived continually by the Holy Breath as the pioneer of our relationship with God.

Day 6

Jesus, Man of Courage

Courage is not simply *one* of the virtues, but the form of every virtue at the testing point, which means, at the point of highest reality.

C. S. LEWIS

But immediately Jesus spoke to them: "Have courage! It is I. Do not be afraid."

MATTHEW 14:27 NET

Although Jesus *felt* fear at times, in the Gospels He mostly appears fearless. He was living a human life, subject to all our temptations, including the temptation to fear, but awareness of God's indwelling presence fueled His courage. Fear never found a foothold in Him.

Courage isn't the absence of fear; it's the ability to do what is right, good, and true even when we feel fear. Courage is the foundational virtue, and Jesus' courage was rooted in knowing His Father was with Him, in Him, and would be the words in His heart and the actions of His hands.

In the Gospels, when others were cowed by the scribes and the Pharisees, Jesus wasn't. He was bluntly honest, even sharp-tongued when necessary, and didn't shy away from truth that could be offensive (Matt. 5:12).

Courage isn't the absence of fear; it's the ability to do what is right, good, and true even when we feel fear.

When the leaders confronted Him, bringing a woman caught in the act of adultery (and where was the man?), they tried to trap Him in front of the crowd: "'Now Moses, in the law, commanded us that such should be stoned. But what do You say?' This they said, testing Him, that they might have something of which to accuse Him. But Jesus stooped down and wrote on the ground with His finger, as though He did not hear" (John 8:5–6).

If He had said to stone her, He would have contradicted His own teachings. "Judge not, and you shall not be judged. Condemn not, and you shall not be condemned. Forgive, and you will be forgiven" (Luke 6:37). If He had said to let her go, the leaders could have accused and tried Him for teaching against the law of Moses.

At first Jesus said nothing, stooping to write in the dust. I wonder if He was buying a little time listening for His Father's voice, or, as some say, writing the Ten Commandments to prepare the Pharisees for what He was going to say next.

When they persisted, Jesus stood and said, "He who is without sin among you, let him throw a stone at her first" (John 8:7).

With masterful composure, Jesus defused the situation in one sentence, saying just the words no one would expect.

Throughout the Gospels we see Jesus "keep His head." He never panicked and always had the perfect thing to say. This composure ran through most of what Jesus said and did. It was there when He was among sick or diseased people; Jesus never ran from sickness. He angered religious people so much they wanted to throw Him off a cliff, but He walked unruffled through their midst (Luke 4:16–30).

Just after His soul-agony in Gethsemane, He stood tall and silent before the Sanhedrin council as they accused and interrogated Him and struck Him in the face. The next morning He came before Pilate, who would soon have Him beaten almost to death and then nailed to a cross. Yet Jesus remained tranquil, a man of few but powerful words.

In Jesus, we see everything good and wonderful a human is meant to be. Courage was a constant foundation of His life and ministry.

In Jesus, we see *everything* good and wonderful a human is meant to be. Courage was a constant foundation of His life and ministry.

In contrast, the disciples often don't show well in the Gospels; they acted from fear, anger, hatred, and self-righteousness. They all fell asleep during the temptation of Jesus in Gethsemane. When Jesus was finally crucified, very few were with Him. Only one of the Twelve was present with the women standing close enough to the cross for Jesus to speak to them (John 19:26).

What was the difference between Jesus and the disciples? What was the source of His courage?

The answer I always heard is that Jesus is God, and the disciples were not. This is true, but the difference is "the Holy Spirit was not yet given [to them], because Jesus was not yet glorified" (John 7:39). Jesus told the disciples, "The Helper, the Holy Spirit, whom the Father will send in My name, He will teach you all things, and bring to your remembrance all things that I said to you" (John 14:26). The indwelling Presence had not yet been sent to the disciples. How can people *trying* to be good by their own human power be like Jesus? Jesus had the courage that flows from living in abiding dependence, while they lived in the illusion of independence and the fear it generates.

Day 7

Another Spirit: The Fire-Breathing Dragon

Now we have received, not the spirit of the world, but the
Spirit who is from God, that we might know the things
that have been freely given to us by God.

1 CORINTHIANS 2:12

The apostle Luke records when Jesus and the disciples were going straight through Samaria on their way to Jerusalem. Samaritans and Jews had a longstanding feud and didn't usually get along, so the Samaritans weren't overly hospitable. They wouldn't allow Jesus and the disciples to stay the night (see Luke 9:51–53). James and John reacted in anger and said to Jesus, "Lord, do You want us to command fire to come down from heaven and consume them, just as Elijah did?" (Luke 9:54).

Condemnation is often our knee-jerk reaction that feels right

43

in the moment. But Jesus, filled with the Holy Breath of God, speaking from the wisdom of His Father, "turned and rebuked them, and said, 'You do not know what manner of spirit you are of'" (Luke 9:55). Their spirit was the fiery breath of a dragon, the spirit of this world. It self-righteously condemns. It's reactive, angry, and punishing.

It's little wonder that these same two disciples who cajoled Jesus to let them rule alongside of Him were the ones most offended when ill-treated (see Mark 10:35–45). Jesus recognized the competing, comparing spirit of this world—the spirit that wants to be at the top of the pile rather than loving and serving others.

After the resurrection and ascension of Jesus, as more and more people were putting their trust in Him, the Pharisee Saul of Tarsus (who was also called Paul) was filled with hatred. Brought up in the Pharisaic traditions, he burned against this new movement that threatened the old ways of Judaism. "Then Saul, still breathing threats and murder against the disciples of the Lord, went to the high priest" (Acts 9:1). Saul was obsessed with rage and ravaged the early church, imprisoning Christians and having many killed.

If we've ever been in a state like that, burning with anger and speaking out wrath and judgment, we know how Saul felt. It's thrilling and horrific, exhilarating and exhausting all in one big, swirling mess. It's dark, and heavy, and oppressive.

It's no wonder this man, being later filled with the Holy Spirit and becoming a great evangelist in the early church, includes in his writings a list of dragon-like behaviors in the "works of the flesh": "hatred, contentions, jealousies, outbursts of wrath, selfish ambitions, dissensions, heresies, envy, murders" (Gal. 5:20–21). He had experienced them all firsthand.

He contrasts the works of the flesh with life in the Spirit: "But the fruit of the Spirit is love, joy, peace, longsuffering, kindness, goodness, faithfulness, gentleness, self-control" (vv. 22–23). Paul wrote to the Corinthians,

> Love suffers long and is kind; love does not envy; love does not parade itself, is not puffed up; does not behave rudely, does not seek its own, is not provoked, thinks no evil; does not rejoice in iniquity, but rejoices in the truth; bears all things, believes all things, hopes all things, endures all things.
>
> Love never fails. (1 Cor. 13:4–8)

We need to pause here and recognize what Paul *doesn't* say: "Love never offends anyone." Jesus, Paul, and the others offended a lot of people, especially anyone who was puffed up with pride.

The gospel tells us we need saving from ourselves, that many of our actions necessitate forgiveness, that we need God's indwelling life to be what we are created to be. This is "the offense of the cross." It means that on our own, no, we are not good enough, strong enough, or loving enough to love others continually with self-giving, wholehearted commitment. *We need God's goodness.*

But Jesus didn't go around being offensive for its own sake. He spoke the truth from loving motives.

Wholehearted commitment to the well-being of another person will sometimes say the hard thing, in a spirit of love, rather than keeping the peace. If we have a friend who is looking up at the clouds, ten feet from tripping over rocks or even walking over a cliff edge, it's not the time to say soft, nice, reassuring words of comfort: "You're doing just fine! Keep on walking authentically! Be who you are!" If we love them, we'd say something like, "Stop! Look! Rocks! Cliff!" We wouldn't want to *affirm* the path they're on; we'd want them first to *look* and then they'd quite naturally want to change direction.

Jesus *listened and paid attention* to the Father, and He said and did what the Father was saying and doing. Sometimes this meant braiding a whip and throwing established, comfortable arrangements tail-over-teakettle.

> *This is* abiding dependence. *To abide is to breathe the air of our true country. As we live in this fresh, clean air, He expands us, gives us an eagle-eye view of people and situations, and fills us with the power to live from His thoughts, His attitudes, and His love.*

Many of Jesus' actions simultaneously transformed some and offended others. A prostitute's life was forever renewed, and her gratitude poured out to Jesus; religious leaders were scandalized because He broke their rule (Luke 7:36–50). A man with a withered arm was healed, his life changed forever; religious leaders were seething because Jesus did a miracle on the wrong day (Mark 3:1–6).

The apostle John wrote, "We have known and believed the love that God has for us. God is love, and he who abides in love abides in God, and God in him" (1 John 4:16). The abiding dependence of Jesus which led Him to love, heal, and change lives also allowed Him to withstand the wrath of the rule-keepers.

Like Jesus, our heart-stance, our thoughts, our attitudes, and our actions are determined by whether we're relying on the Holy Breath. This is *abiding dependence*. To abide is to breathe the air of our true country. As we live in this fresh, clean air, He expands us, gives us an eagle-eye view of people and situations, and fills us with the power to live from His thoughts, His attitudes, and His love.

Without reliance, without fellowship with God, without abiding, we'll be breathing the wrong air, the spirit of fear, judgment, and condemnation. Jesus said, "Do not judge according to appearance, but judge with righteous judgment" (John 7:24).

Day 8

The Abiding
Dependence of Jesus

Christ said in the fifth chapter of John that He had no
independent life of His own but was constantly
dependent on His Father for every word and act.... So
He wants you and me to live by Him. He is just repeating
the life He lived when He trod the hills of Galilee: utterly
dependent, an empty vessel, receiving all from above.
So, now, He requires you and me to be empty vessels,
receiving all from Him.

A. B. SIMPSON

Remember when I said, "*Dependence* on His indwelling Father is the biggest identifying stamp of the earthly life of Jesus Christ"? Jesus had to *know* His Father as living, speaking, and working inside Him, moving all around Him through people and situations. He waited and listened, consciously recognizing His Father as His source of everything. It was *habitual,* continual contact with the life, love, power, and wisdom of His Father.

The central *work* of Jesus as He lived His daily life was to rest in and to *stay with* the Father. Jesus held to an attitude of reliance, of abiding, the Father in the Son and the Son in the Father; He breathed, lived, spoke, and moved as one with His Father.

> "Do you not believe that I am in the Father, and the Father in Me? The words that I speak to you I do not speak on My own authority; but the Father who dwells in Me does the works. Believe Me that I am in the Father and the Father in Me, or else believe Me for the sake of the works themselves." (John 14:10–11)

Jesus knew His own humanity could accomplish *nothing* of any lasting value without His Father abiding in Him and He in His Father: "I can of Myself do nothing" (John 5:30).

Jesus held to an attitude of reliance, of abiding, the Father in the Son and the Son in the Father; He breathed, lived, spoke, and moved as one with His Father.

This intimate union was the source of all of His words and works: "For the Father loves the Son, and shows Him all things that He Himself does; and He will show Him greater works than these, that you may marvel" (John 5:20).

Being Father-dependent meant Jesus didn't have the need to *control* others—to manipulate. He never worked to convince people to join Him and didn't chase after followers who left. We see an example of this in Mark: "Now as He was going out on the road, one came running, knelt before Him, and asked Him, 'Good Teacher, what shall I do that I may inherit eternal life?'" (Mark 10:17). Jesus put His finger on the one thing weighing the young man down: his money. He responded, "One thing you lack: Go your way, sell whatever you have and give to the poor, and you will have treasure in heaven; and come, take up the cross, and follow Me" (Mark 10:21).

Though the young ruler "was sad at this word, and went away sorrowful, for he had great possessions" (Mark 10:22), Jesus didn't run after him, argue, or change His position; He let the young man go away sad, still in bondage to his possessions.

Jesus seldom spoke angry words, but there are a few instances. The scribes and Pharisees were so deeply entrenched in their religious tradition they didn't have ears to hear His teaching, and they didn't want anyone else to hear Him either. Jesus rebuked them, "But woe to you, scribes and Pharisees, hypocrites! For you shut up the kingdom of heaven against men; for you neither go in yourselves, nor do you allow those who are entering to go in" (Matt. 23:13).

How we see God is something He takes seriously. The religious leaders loved their positions of power, even under Roman rule, and they were afraid of losing those positions and their nation. They said, "If we let Him alone like this, everyone will believe in Him, and the Romans will come and take away both our place and nation" (John 11:48).

Jesus said in scathing critique, "But all their works they do to be seen by men. . . . They love the best places at feasts, the best seats in the synagogues, greetings in the marketplaces, and to be called by men, 'Rabbi, Rabbi.' . . . Woe to you, scribes and Pharisees, hypocrites! For you devour widows' houses, and for a pretense make long prayers" (Matt. 23:5–7, 14).

Jesus contrasted their good works, done to be applauded, with the relationship and fellowship of abiding dependence, telling His disciples, "But you, when you pray, go into your room, and when you have shut your door, pray to your Father who is in the secret place; and your Father who sees in secret will reward you openly" (Matt. 6:6).

The Pharisees were suppressing the good news of relationship and closeness with God to ensure their continued positions of power, benefits, and the continued survival of their people. They were operating from fear, pride, and independence, acting more like wolves than shepherds.

Jesus lived in abiding dependence, and the Spirit of God powered His humanity. He became one of us so we could become like Him, living and walking in a union-relationship with God. "For He made Him who knew no sin to be sin for us, that we might become the righteousness of God in Him" (2 Cor. 5:21).

Day 9

Jesus the Reconciler

God was in Christ reconciling the world to Himself, not
imputing their trespasses to them, and has committed to
us the word of reconciliation.

2 CORINTHIANS 5:19

If we have a friend we love who misunderstands us, believing
lies and separating themselves from us, we go to them. To restore
the relationship, we humble ourselves. We ask ourselves, "What
can I do to restore our friendship?" And then we go say and do
whatever needs to be done to clear the air.

Paul writes, "God was in Christ reconciling the world to
Himself." This doesn't say God was reconciling Himself to the
world; He was reconciling the world to Himself. Paul continues,
"as though God were pleading through us: we implore you on
Christ's behalf, be reconciled to God" (2 Cor. 5:20).

God humbled Himself in Jesus to become kin with us. He came
to offer Himself because He wants *us* to be reconciled to *Him.*

To illustrate this, Jesus told the story of the prodigal son (Luke 15:11–32). The younger son from a wealthy family asked for his inheritance, went away, and wasted it all. All the wild parties, being the cool guy, the hungover mornings, the prostitutes—he tried to get identity from anything other than his father's love and authority. As the money ran out and his false identity crashed, his equally false friends deserted him. Without relationship and fellowship with his father, the resources that at first seemed limitless ran out. He felt powerless. Stress and anxiety ruled his days.

The father of the prodigal wasn't waiting at home trying to reconcile himself to his son or what he had done. The father's acceptance, love, forgiveness, and resources were waiting for the prodigal all the time, but only became available to him the moment he came home. We can't be handed a steady daily inflow without being near the Hand.

When the son came home, the father ran to him, rejoicing, immediately affirming him as an heir by giving him a robe, a ring, and sandals—covering, authority, and a share in the family work. Then the father threw a joyous party.

The father gave no punishment, which would have shocked the religious minds of the day. The father didn't even say, "Well, I hope you've learned your lesson." He didn't begrudge the wasted money or chastise the son in any way.

At the end of the story, the only one unreconciled was the older brother. He certainly *was* shocked by his father's unbridled love and generosity. He clung to unforgiveness, was self-righteous, and told his father,

> "Lo, these many years I have been serving you; I never transgressed your commandment at any time; and yet you never

gave me a young goat, that I might make merry with my friends. But as soon as this son of yours came, who has devoured your livelihood with harlots, you killed the fatted calf for him." (Luke 15:29–30)

The elder son's underlying attitude was, *I work to be worthy and accepted, and to gain access to my father's resources.* Love, worth, and acceptance came from his performance. He served dutifully to get what he wanted. This mindset sets up the comparison game where others are less worthy. It made him self-righteous.

The younger was sure his father would disown him and make him into a hired hand; after all, he had been bad and *deserved* punishment. His concept of love, worth, and acceptance also came from his performance. Neither son knew the father's heart; both believed acceptance was conditional. But the younger still had the father's love while eating from the pig trough. He couldn't experience the love, forgiveness, joy, patience, kindness, or the resources of his father until he went home.

The father said to the elder, "Son, you are always with me, and all that I have is yours" (Luke 15:31). He didn't have to earn his father's presence or his resources. At home, living in relationship, the Father's resources are *our own* resources. They're freely given and can be freely used. But the elder couldn't experience the joyfulness of fellowship with his father until he found his real home in his father's heart.

They had to *know* their father and how he thought of them to turn their minds, hearts, attitudes, and actions to being co-heirs rather than mere servants. They both needed to be reconciled to their father and to one another. Their father wasn't against them; he was continually giving to them and was *for* them.

Being reconciled to God is a divine trade. We go home to the heart of God, and God makes His home in us wherever we go. Jesus said, "If anyone loves Me, he will keep My word; and My Father will love him, and We will come to him and make Our home with him" (John 14:23). From the prodigal's return onward, he carried his father with him—his father's love, his power, his authority, his resources. Responsible behavior flowed out of going home, being reconciled to the *relationship*, and having fellowship restored.

> *Being reconciled to God is a divine trade. We go home to the heart of God, and God makes His home in us wherever we go.*

There will be no flow of resources without our reconciliation to God, without coming to Him in fellowship. We eventually burn out. Like the father in the story, God is full of joy when He sees us moving on the road toward Him (Luke 15:7). God loves for us to realize He is for us, not against us. He wants us home.

Come home and be filled. God is not against you; He is for you. If you're the prodigal son—running on empty, thinking you have to "clean up your life" before you come back, believing if you return, you'll be second-class with God—take His joy, His ring, His robe, and His sandals. Be reconciled to God; He has never stopped loving you, and His forgiveness is always waiting for you right where you sit. You don't have to clean up your life before you come to God. Fellowship with Him will clean you and change you.

If you're the elder brother, religious, dutiful, always serious, sometimes resentful, take part in the Father's joy and join His celebration. You don't need to earn anything; you can loosen up and live a little. As C. S. Lewis wrote, "Everything is here for the asking and nothing can be bought."[1] You already have the Father's love and approval by being a son or daughter. *Be reconciled.*

Day 10

What the Humanity of Jesus Means for Us

"Do you not believe that I am in the Father, and the Father in Me? ... A little while longer and the world will see Me no more, but you will see Me. Because I live, you will live also. At that day you will know that I am in My Father, and you in Me, and I in you."

JOHN 14:10, 19-20

I grew up with the impression I had to stuff my feelings and strive to be more kind or loving like Jesus, or have faith like David, or be full of zeal like Paul. They were heroes I was supposed to emulate. But platitudes like "Be more loving" and "Have faith" have no power for someone believing love, faith, and other qualities depend on their *own* effort and willpower. We may as well tell a rock to dance as say to an angry person, "Be more loving," or to the depressed, "Try to have more faith."

The gospel goes much deeper than feelings or behavior; it is deeper than who we *think* we are. The good news flows down to our self-concept, soaking into the hard places where our self-image is at odds with our true, God-given identity in Christ.

C. S. Lewis wrote, "God made us: invented us as a man invents an engine. A car is made to run on petrol, and it would not run properly on anything else. Now God designed the human machine to run on Himself. He Himself is the fuel our spirits were designed to burn, or the food our spirits were designed to feed on. There is no other."[1]

The life of the Father in Jesus flowed through His attitude of childlike dependence; Jesus had strong emotions, but His Father held the reins of His heart.

> *The good news flows down to our self-concept, soaking into the hard places where our self-image is at odds with our true, God-given identity in Christ.*

The disciples asked, "Who then is greatest in the kingdom of heaven?" Jesus put a little child in the midst of them and said, "Assuredly, I say to you, unless you are converted and become as little children, you will by no means enter the kingdom of heaven. Therefore whoever humbles himself as this little child is the greatest in the kingdom of heaven" (Matt. 18:1–4).

The disciples wanted an answer to boost their self-dependence, but Jesus pointed them to the humble trust of a child. He was asked, "How can we, too, work the works of God?" and He answered, "This is the work of God, that you believe in Him whom He sent" (John 6:29). He pointed them to reliant trust, abiding dependence, as central.

Being named "greatest in the kingdom of heaven" isn't determined by achievement, but by one single, tiny thing. It's something the weakest of us can do at any moment: we can depend on God with the humble heart of a little child.

After the resurrection, the disciples had the same personalities, but they reacted and responded differently than before. The biggest change was the courage they had in the book of Acts after receiving the Holy Spirit in chapter 2. The once brash and impulsive Peter boldly and spontaneously preached a sermon, bringing three thousand people to their knees and into the kingdom. In Acts 3, he and John healed a man who couldn't walk, and when people around them were amazed, staring at them, Peter preached another sermon, beginning with, "Men of Israel, why do you marvel at this? Or why look so intently at us, as though by our own power or godliness we had made this man walk?" (Acts 3:12). This was the man who used to boast about his own ability and denied knowing Jesus three times just weeks earlier, terrified of servants around a fire. After Pentecost he was full of courage, acting on impulse from the Holy Spirit, and boasting in Christ.

To again quote Lewis, "Courage is not simply *one* of the virtues, but the form of every virtue at the testing point, which means, at the point of highest reality. A chastity or honesty, or mercy, which yields to danger will be chaste or honest or merciful only on conditions. Pilate was merciful until it became risky."[2]

The disciples now had the Holy Spirit, a living relationship and fellowship with God for themselves, through Christ. They finally began to understand Jesus' words: "I am the vine, you are the branches. He who abides in Me, and I in him, bears much fruit; for without Me you can do nothing" (John 15:5). As they lived in abiding dependence, their personalities were now coming under the rule of the Spirit, and courage was the first result.

How does dependence look in everyday situations? In an argument, we'll have our internal emotional reactions. But we can practice silently taking a moment to recognize God as present, that He is working in and upon us, and in the other person—that we are not alone, independent, striving to make our life work, that we don't have to manipulate or control. God is love in us, and we can joyfully expect Him to love through us and give us truthful, loving words to say. We "cast our cares on Him," and He gives us the peace that brings courage.

"Courage is not simply one of the virtues, but the form of every virtue at the testing point."
—C. S. Lewis

When we wake up at three o'clock in the morning with our minds dredging up some foolish thing we've said or done and already repented of in the past, feeling self-condemnation and shame, we take a moment to breathe, recognizing and thanking God for His presence. He is the Redeemer. We can think it through with Him; He will redeem it all, use it for good purposes, and teach us better ways to respond for next time (see Rom. 8:28).

The other spirit wants us to stuff our feelings and imitate the external actions of Jesus by our own human strength and effort. It works from guilt, fear, and self-condemnation. It's constantly whispering, "You should have been better. Try harder. Be more like Jesus." It keeps score, compares, and judges others.

God wants spiritual *fruition*, not fleshly imitation. As branches in the vine, we don't generate fruit; we bear it. When we practice depending and relying on God, acknowledging our emotions to Him, sap begins to flow into our thoughts, our attitudes, and our actions. Excessive emotions begin to dissipate. Fruit appears.

These things are *practiced*. It's not instantaneous; we mature in it. We're pilgrims, walking through this world, and we sometimes trip, fall, and get up again. Jesus is the Way, the road, the path we travel day by day. Abiding dependence is a walk with God more than a quick-fix formula.

Our basic personalities remain, but over time they become redirected toward what is beneficial to ourselves and others. Abiding dependence brings God's life, fruit, and action through our humanity as we trust, listen, and follow the guidance of the Holy Spirit in us—God in us, with us, and through us.

Day 11

The Serpent
on the Pole

"As Moses lifted up the serpent in the wilderness, even so
must the Son of Man be lifted up, that whoever believes
in Him should not perish but have eternal life."

JOHN 3:14-15

The Pharisee Nicodemus came to Jesus one night to ask some
honest questions. He had a hard time understanding what Jesus
was teaching, so Jesus pointed him to something Nicodemus had
studied his whole life—a passage in Numbers 21, when the Hebrews were in the wilderness. Moses had led them out of slavery
in Egypt, and God had shown them many miraculous demon-
strations of His power, love, and care, including providing manna
every morning. As they camped out in tents, the people continued their discontented grumbling with every setback; soon their
grumbling ill tempers exploded:

> The soul of the people became very discouraged on the way. And
> the people spoke against God and against Moses: "Why have
> you brought us up out of Egypt to die in the wilderness? For
> there is no food and no water, and our soul loathes this worth-
> less bread." So the LORD sent fiery serpents among the people,
> and they bit the people; and many of the people of Israel died.
> (Num. 21:4–6)

The symbol is fitting; the spirit that boiled in their hearts was the same poisonous breath James and John showed in wanting to call down fire on the Samaritans and Peter had when he wanted to prevent Jesus from going to the cross.

The Hebrews realized they'd been ungrateful and blasphemous, and they asked Moses to pray for the serpents to be taken away. The Lord responded to Moses's prayer, "'Make a fiery serpent, and set it on a pole; and it shall be that everyone who is bitten, when he looks at it, shall live.' So Moses made a bronze serpent, and put it on a pole; and so it was, if a serpent had bitten anyone, when he looked at the bronze serpent, he lived" (Num. 21:8–9). The serpents weren't taken away, but a cure was given.

As Jesus sat with Nicodemus and reminded him of this story, He showed how the serpent on a pole was a symbol or shadow of the true reality, that He would *become* sin for us on the cross. Jesus said "that whoever believes *in Him* should not perish but have everlasting life" (John 3:16). He didn't say, "Whoever agrees that His sacrifice paid the penalty for sin." Jesus said we are to believe, trust, rely, put all our faith *in Him*, in Jesus, the Son of God, the person—not in an idea, a concept, a doctrine, or by intellectually assenting to the truth of His sacrifice.

George MacDonald wrote, "No manner or amount of belief

about him is the faith of the New Testament. With such teaching I have had a lifelong acquaintance, and declare it most miserably false . . . the trusting in anything but himself, his own living self, is a delusion."[1]

The Hebrews were told to look at the serpent on the pole, to see it, consider it, regard it, to trust they would be healed from the bite of the serpent. Jesus wants us to *see, consider, regard,* to trust *in Him,* the one who became sin for us. To trust Jesus requires the closeness of fellowship. We find Him trustworthy and reliable through experiencing who He is. And yes, it also means we learn many things *about* Him, and it means we believe what He has done for us, but we put our faith, our trust, in *Him.* We are to look at and trust Jesus Himself, to depend on Him.

The self-dependence of the Hebrews was a Pandora's box of fears, producing grumbling, manipulation, wrath, and all the rest. The poisonous snakes were a symbol of the spiritual serpent with its fangs buried deep in their hearts.

Jesus ate our death so that we might live His life.

This is the spirit, the breath of the fall in the garden of Eden. If we look at history or at the current state of our world, we can easily see its effects on our human race.

Jesus bore this poison on the cross, becoming the receptacle of not only the sins of humanity—the actions—but of the poison of sin itself, the spirit of sin. He not only took on our humanity in life, with all its feelings and temptations; He also brought *us* into Himself, into His death, with our illusion of independent life and dependence on the lies of the serpent. Jesus took into

Himself what would have been our despairing cry, "My God, My God, why have You forsaken Me?" to give us a joyful cry: "For you did not receive the spirit of bondage again to fear, but you received the Spirit of adoption by whom we cry out, 'Abba, Father'" (Rom 8:15).

Jesus ate our death so that we might live His life. "I have come that they may have life, and that they may have it more abundantly" (John 10:10). We can choose to breathe the air of heaven here and now, because Jesus took on Himself our hell of self-dependence and its results—fear, sin, and our daily hells— on the cross.

Day 12

What the Cross Means for Us

For He made Him who knew no sin to be sin for us, that
we might become the righteousness of God in Him.

2 CORINTHIANS 5:21

The night before He was executed, Jesus told the disciples, "If
you love Me, keep My commandments. And I will pray the Father, and He will give you another Helper, that He may abide with
you forever—the Spirit of truth, whom the world cannot receive,
because it neither sees Him nor knows Him; but you know Him,
for He dwells with you and will be in you. I will not leave you
orphans; I will come to you" (John 14:15–18).

The Holy Spirit wasn't going to live only in Jesus; He was coming to indwell a vast family of sons and daughters of God all over
the world from every race, language, and region.

Major Ian Thomas wrote, "Christ did not die simply that you

might be saved from a bad conscience, or even to remove the stain of past failure, but to 'clear the decks' for His divine activity through you."[1]

The cross is where the life of Jesus collides with our identity. Our old self died in Him.

Many of us grew up hearing sermons about "the old self." The idea is often hazy in our minds. We rarely define "the old self."

Paul defines it in Ephesians 2, where he says we were "dead in trespasses and sins, in which you once walked according to the course of this world, according to the prince of the power of the air, the spirit who now works in the sons of disobedience" (Eph. 2:1–2). The old self was our human personality in a union, a marriage, with a different spirit. We were branches in a false vine, thinking we were independent. We weren't. We followed the desires of our bodies and souls, the fears and opinions of others, and formed our identity from what people thought of us. We practiced good works and religion to feel good about ourselves in a world of performance-based acceptance. We followed the lies of the tempter.

At the cross, we were immersed into His death so that we could come alive with Him in His resurrection. Jesus severed that old union and united us with Himself. We are no longer under the principle that brings only sin and death—the illusion of independence.[2]

Paul says we're to live in a new reality: "For the death that He died, He died to sin once for all; but the life that He lives, He lives to God. Likewise you also, reckon yourselves to be dead indeed to sin, but alive to God in Christ Jesus our Lord" (Rom. 6:10–11). Paul says to consider it fact that just as Jesus hung dead on the cross, just as they took His lifeless body down to bury it, so we died to sin and are unified with God—as we would count it as a fact that the sky is blue. We are in a new marriage union with the Spirit of God (see Rom. 7:4).

This often brings up an obvious question. If the old self is dead, why do we still sin? For the moment, let's ask ourselves this: Have I attempted in any way to do what Paul told me to do? Have I ever consistently counted myself dead to sin, but alive to God, as an act of faith and gut-level trust? Or do I find ways to wriggle around it theologically?

One of my pastors used to say, "There's no freedom in a vacuum. The drunkard isn't free; he's enslaved to his drink. The sex addict isn't free; he's enslaved to his body." The Hebrews in the wilderness weren't free; they were slaves to fear, whims, grumbling, and their own desires. As God's people, we can still choose to live in the illusion of independence. In doing so we give ourselves in submission to anything and everything but God. The result is fear, sin, shame—walking in a living hell. But that's not who we really are.

Our new identity is dependent on our union with Christ through the eternal love and goodness of God. Everything we need for life and godliness is inside us in Christ, waiting to be unpacked by trust and reliance.

As Paul explains, "put off your old self, which belongs to your former manner of life and is corrupt through deceitful desires, and . . . be renewed in the spirit of your minds, and . . . put on the new self, created after the likeness of God in true righteousness and holiness" (Eph. 4:22–24 ESV).

What does it mean to put off the old self and put on the new? I used to think I had to try harder to be good by my own effort, or, at best, with the Holy Spirit "helping me."

Rather, it means the ways of thinking, the attitudes, and the actions of the old self, imprinted on us by the old union, no longer fit us. We take up our cross, recognize we died to all that, and take a new, daily attitude of being alive to God as new creations in Christ, as branches in the vine. We put on new, God-dependent ways of thinking, new attitudes about God, ourselves, and others. We *recognize and remember* God is real, present, and in us in every situation. A fruit-of-the-Spirit life begins and continues with abiding dependence.

How do these new attitudes work out in daily life? As we interact with others, we can remember God sees every single situation from a different vantage point. He sees how we were raised, what's happened to us, knows our disappointments, our fears, our anxieties. He's the only One who knows everything about us. And He knows all about the other person, too.

In having direct, inner access to God, we can silently ask Him for clarity, wisdom, understanding, and deep insight into the other person, so we see from His much higher, wider, and more loving vantage point. When I recognize the reality and presence of God with me and in me, my fears begin to abate. God is in me, giving me peace, wisdom, and an ability to really listen to the heart of the other person. Love flows up into me for them. He's also in them, prompting them to truly hear. God may have some things He wants me to say—but maybe not. He just may have some things I need to hear.

Practicing this fellowship with God as a habit and learning to see Him as a constant presence, guide, and companion calms our storms, heals our blind spots, and gives us ears to hear.

The old independent mindset doesn't take God into account. Independence mires us in our old, limited, small ways of thinking as we live from the wrong spirit and attitude. When we forget to abide, we soon revert to our defaults.

New-man thinking says, "I am a reborn child of God, a new creation. The old has gone, and the new has come. I have a God who is always present with me and in me. I depend on Him, His love for me, His life in me, His resources, His love for everyone in my circle of influence. God lives inside me, through Christ, by the Holy Spirit. My being is now alive to God."

Practicing this fellowship with God as a habit and learning to see Him as a constant presence, guide, and companion calms our storms, heals our blind spots, and gives us ears to hear.

We take up our cross by embracing this new reality. Our thoughts and feelings will often rebel: "Why *should* I forgive him? I was in the right!" We'll often hear every possible reason in our heads why we shouldn't lay down our lives, why we should win the argument at all costs, why our present temptation is more important, more powerful, and more necessary than God's power in us to "Take up your cross and follow Me."

If we want to experience renewal and resurrection, we must take up our cross. We lay down the old and put on the new.

Day 13

Resurrection

Therefore we have been buried with him through bap-
tism into death, in order that just as Christ was raised
from the dead through the glory of the Father,
so we too may live a new life.
For if we have become united with him in the likeness
of his death, we will certainly also be united in the
likeness of his resurrection.

ROMANS 6:4–5 NET

The apostle Paul brings the resurrection of Jesus into our everyday lives. When the Holy Spirit reanimated the dead body of
Jesus (Rom. 8:11), we were raised to walk in a new kind of life—
now. The apostle Paul says, "Therefore if anyone is in Christ, he
is a new creation; old things have passed away; behold, all things
have become new" (2 Cor. 5:17). We've become a new kind of
being that has never existed before; we're in Christ, and Christ is
in us.

This extremely good news means I don't have to live from my

own resources, my own willpower, my own human effort, my own trying. If I lay down "my life"—what I think I want, what I think I need—I get a flow of resurrection-life.

Paul explains in Romans 7 how we died to living from our own effort and willpower. He uses marriage as a symbol of our union with Christ and says we died to our old husband—the law, the principle that since God has a standard of righteousness, we're to keep it by *trying hard*, and that this trying will make us holy. We were married to this spirit of independence and willpower.

If you've ever tried too hard to be good at something, you'll recognize that there is something about the underlying fear of not being sufficient for the job that makes you try harder. The trying "puts you off your game." It doesn't allow for easy, natural movement, smooth conversation, or truly funny jokes. You become stifled because you're self-conscious and too focused on doing everything "right."

A Christian "trying to be like Jesus" has the same problem.

Paul says the law, "Do not covet," produced in him all manner of coveting by awakening a sin-consciousness (Rom. 7:7–12). It got him focused on sin and he tried to quell it by his own willpower and effort. Self-effort produces sin because we become focused on sin-avoidance. A branch trying to produce fruit by its own ability cuts itself off from the source and withers. This is how Paul can say that the law was given to make offenses increase (Rom. 5:20) and that the power of sin comes from the law (1 Cor. 15:56). The law stimulates the tendency to self-dependence and pride, and we disconnect from abiding in Christ. The result is sin (1 John 3:6).

The law wasn't given to make us holy; it was given to expose independence, self-effort, and pride. It was given to *increase* offenses and ultimately to drive us to the true source of goodness.

From Romans 7:7 to verse 24, where Paul is outlining this dilemma of fleshly effort, he never mentions the Holy Spirit, Christ, or God. In this "trying" passage, Paul continually references himself, using "I," "me," and "my" over *forty times*. Only in verse 25, and into Romans 8, does his emphasis change to the Holy Spirit.

If you're in the jungle with a man-eating tiger roaming around, all your thoughts focus on avoiding it. When you're spending all your time and thought avoiding a tiger, there's no time to think of anything but your own problem.

As a musician I'm not going to play my best if my focus is on avoiding mistakes. I'll be too safe and careful in my performance, and it's likely, because of fear and misplaced focus, that I'll make more mistakes. I'm playing from fear rather than being powered by the love of making music. To play well, I have to cast off fear, step into trust, and play from a sense of sufficiency. To truly fulfill any of God's law toward my neighbors, I must rise higher than sin-avoidance and fastidious rule-keeping; I must live from love. If I love them, I won't steal or covet or lie.

> *Love isn't generated by me trying to love. I need something higher than my human love and strength—I need to live from the eternal love of God.*

But here's the problem: there's only one continually flowing source of love—God (1 John 4:8). Love isn't generated by me *trying* to love. I need something higher than my human love and strength—I need to live from the eternal love of God.

Paul prays "that the God of our Lord Jesus Christ, the Father of glory, may give to you the spirit of wisdom and revelation in the knowledge of Him, the eyes of your understanding being enlightened; that you may know what is the hope of His calling, what are the riches of the glory of His inheritance in the saints, and what is the *exceeding greatness of His power toward us who believe, according to the working of His mighty power*" (Eph. 1:17–19).

In the new covenant we are filled with this resurrection power. The old way is flipped upside down, and holiness now doesn't depend on my self-fueled human effort. The Ten Commandments become ten promises. I'll have no other gods before me because Christ in me protects me. I'll love God with all my heart, soul, mind, and strength because Christ in me is the very love of God. I'll love my neighbor as myself because the Holy Spirit in me is a never-ending river of God's love. The commandments become diagnostic; if I'm turning food or drink or sex or entertainment or anything else into a little god to get relief every time I feel stress and anxiety, if I'm envious and coveting, if I'm telling "white lies" to stay out of trouble or not take responsibility, then I'm not depending on, trusting in, or living from the Holy Spirit in me. God's life in me is blocked by my unbelief.

The apostle Paul wrote to the Philippians, "Being confident of this very thing, that He who has begun a good work in you will complete it until the day of Jesus Christ" (Phil. 1:6). God begins the good work, and God completes the good work. Our part is to abide and depend.

Our new life begins to awaken when we practice laying down "my life"—"my rights" and "what I deserve"—and recognize Him as real, present, and within us. We are *in Him*, and in every circumstance and for every situation, "His divine power has given to us all things that pertain to life and godliness, through the knowledge of Him who called us by glory and virtue" (2 Peter 1:3). This is abiding dependence, and when we take up the cross and lay down our lives in trust, living in His life—His forgiving, loving, reconciling life—the result is resurrection.

Day 14

Grace and Law

> Let me ask you this one question: Did you receive the
> Holy Spirit by obeying the law of Moses? Of course not!
> You received the Spirit because you believed the message
> you heard about Christ. How foolish can you be? After
> starting your new lives in the Spirit, why are you now
> trying to become perfect by your own human effort?
>
> GALATIANS 3:2-3 NLT

Paul's letter to the Galatians was dashed off in a passion because the Galatians were listening to legalistic teachers pointing
them back to their own independent human power. They were
teaching that Jesus died so our sins could be forgiven, but that
we've got to add our human effort to that—as if we've got to *try* to
keep rules in order to really be accepted and empowered by God.
They were teaching that salvation—deliverance from sin—came
by the grace and forgiveness of God *plus* our human-fueled effort.

They wanted to mix grace—the loving, forgiving, empower-
ing life and favor of God in us—with independent self-effort.

In case the Holy Spirit couldn't get the job done, or if God forgot, they were going to make sure everyone tried hard. But a Christian "try-er" is, at best, a person with a divided mind. One moment we're looking to God for forgiveness and to get us to heaven when we die, and in the next we're assessing our own ability, critiquing our performance, and comparing ourselves to others. There is never the full-hearted, bet-the-farm attitude, seeing and trusting God for everything. A double-minded person is unstable in all their ways (James 1:8).

Paul said to the Galatians, "I am crucified with Christ: nevertheless I live; yet not I, but Christ liveth in me: and the life which I now live in the flesh I live by the faith of the Son of God, who loved me, and gave himself for me" (Gal. 2:20 KJV). Paul continually recognized the source of his life, love, and power. That source was inside Paul, but it wasn't Paul. Paul didn't even live from his own faith; it was the faith of the Spirit of Christ inside him. Even faith is a fruit of the Spirit listed in Galatians 5:22.

Pulling back from reliance on God to operate in independent, self-willed power—trying to complete or mature ourselves by our own human effort—is the most foolish thing we can do. "Christ is become of no effect unto you, whosoever of you are justified by the law; ye are fallen from grace" (Gal. 5:4 KJV).

A Christian "try-er" is, at best, a person with a divided mind.

Christ in us is rendered idle, deactivated, and inoperative the moment we attempt to justify ourselves by trying hard to be good. We fall from grace—from living in the love, favor, and sanctifying power of God—back into self-effort. You can't walk east and west at the same time. At best, you can alternate between going east and west, but you won't get very far walking like that.

In Galatians, Paul refers to God's promise to Abram in Genesis, "I will make you a great nation" (Gen. 12:2). Abram's wife Sarai was unable to have children. Decades passed, and still they had no son. Wanting Abram to have an heir, her faith in God's promise failing, Sarai thought up her own plan. "'See now, the LORD has restrained me from bearing children. Please, go in to my maid; perhaps I shall obtain children by her.' And Abram heeded the voice of Sarai" (Gen. 16:2).

Sarai's servant Hagar bore Abram's child, Ishmael, born not by God fulfilling His promise, but by Abram's and Sarai's fleshly plan that came from their own limited viewpoint. God wasn't getting the job done quickly enough, so Abram and Sarai decided to help Him out.

The Galatians were going back to thinking like Sarai and Abram, trying to help God fulfill His promises rather than trusting and depending on Him.

We can live from His indwelling power *or* believe life comes from our willpower and independent self-effort—but we can't have both. Grace and self-effort don't mix. It's either-or. We are either abiding in Christ, seeing Him, recognizing Him, knowing Him, and living from Him, or we're living by our own fleshly effort.

A few months after leaving a legalistic church I attended for a year as a teen, I was sitting in my friend Eric's Volkswagen after a band rehearsal, pouring my heart out. Eric patiently listened. One of the things he said was, "Ron, we're not saved by what we do or don't do. We're saved by *trusting God.*" It was my single most defining moment as a teen.

Trust and dependence are core issues, and through knowing

God in fellowship they deepen and strengthen. Knowing we're forgiven and going to heaven someday isn't the same as trusting, resting, and abiding daily. Major Ian Thomas preached, "The knowledge that He died for you and your sins are forgiven because He died for you, in itself, does not impart to you any new spiritual caliber of living. And if all that Jesus Christ did when He came to this world 1,900 years ago was to live that sinless life to qualify Him for that redeeming death and then go straight back to Heaven and simply wait till you got there—that wouldn't be much of a salvation. It would be a salvation that made you fit for Heaven and left you hopelessly inadequate for earth."[1]

Jesus delivers us from ways of life that darken or distort our personalities, shipwreck our relationships, destroy our lives, or worse, ways that fool us into thinking they are "life."

The salvation Jesus offers doesn't stop with mere forgiveness and a clean start; He delivers us from ways of life that darken or distort our personalities, shipwreck our relationships, destroy our lives, or worse, ways that fool us into thinking they are "life"—putting religion, "success," possessions, "being an influencer," or even ministry over relationship and fellowship with God.

Jesus came to give us His own life right here and now. He came to be our present-tense Deliverer. What He requires from us is honesty and reliant trust.

Forgiveness is only the entrance to the gate at the edge of the property on the driveway up to the great mansion of what "being saved" really means. At some point we need to go up and explore this mansion to experience what happens when we live daily, moment by moment, with God.

Day 15

Belief Often Determines Experience

If you will not believe, surely you shall not be established.

ISAIAH 7:9

God made the one who did not know sin
to be sin for us, so that in him we would
become the righteousness of God.

2 CORINTHIANS 5:21 NET

Jesus was born, lived, died, and rose so that in Him we would become the righteousness of God—that the love of God, the peace of God, the joy of God, would spill out of us into our everyday lives to other people.

Many have spun this righteousness into a "someday" mentality; that someday when we die we'll be made righteous, that righteousness is our *position* in Christ but can't be our *experience*. We've constructed elaborate theologies to explain why we don't experience the life described in the New Testament, and as a result we end up "having the appearance of godliness, but denying its power" (2 Tim. 3:5 ESV).

Yet our experience is often determined by what we believe is possible. When Jesus was in His hometown, "He did not do many mighty works there because of their unbelief" (Matt. 13:58).

Romans 8 says, "Therefore, brethren, we are debtors—not to the flesh, to live according to the flesh. For if you live according to the flesh you will die; but if by the Spirit you put to death the deeds of the body, you will live. For as many as are led by the Spirit of God, these are sons of God" (Rom. 8:12–14). In the Greek, "you will die" is in the present tense—it's a walking death, more like, "You will be dying." And isn't it that way when we're walking independently, trying to make our life work? We get tangled up, frustrated with people and situations, and then we self-medicate to try to get enough of a mental rest to try harder tomorrow—a living death.

Now, follow my human reasoning here for a moment. If I want to become a better guitarist, I must first *want* it. I can't just intellectually assent to the idea of it being possible. I have to want it and also *actively trust* it is possible. Then I have to step out on that trust and *do*.

If I *sort of* believe it's possible to get better, *maybe, probably not*, then that's going to dampen my doing. I'll procrastinate, inconsistently working toward my musical goals, and a year later I'll say, "See? I'm just not talented enough." The real problem wouldn't be talent; it would be in lack of desire, or in believing that change is impossible. In music, as in sports, attitude is everything. The questions are, "Do you want it? Do you believe it's possible?" Then we leap out in trust.

If I believe—not just intellectually, but consistently *trust*—that it's possible to become a better guitarist, then I have the necessary energy and focus to move toward that goal, persevering in hope. That sort of faith sometimes means digging up the weeds of old beliefs and throwing them on the burn pile. It means taking time occasionally to think about what we want and why we want it.

To move toward living the life of the Spirit in our everyday lives, we must first *desire* it. If you didn't desire to love God and others, to grow, to become everything you are meant to be, if you're satisfied with yourself and your life just as it is, or if you believed there's no way to be better, you probably wouldn't be reading this book. You'd simply be uninterested, and you might think this was all soul-butter and hogwash.

But since you're still reading, I assume you've got the desire. The next essential step is to trust, to begin to know deep down it's possible to have a daily life of walking with God, living in the Spirit, having love, joy, peace, patience, and all the fruit of the Spirit— because you already have Him inside you.

If I repeat, "I am a lousy, terrible guitarist" in my heart of hearts, over and over for years, make no mistake—lo and behold, the thing will come to pass. When I'm believing life depends wholly on *me*, on my trying harder, on my limited abilities, I live in fear, stress, and tension. Overfocus on mistakes creates more mistakes.

An overfocus on "I am a sinner," a continual expectation of sin, and the resulting self-condemnation dishonors and downplays the love, life, and power God has given to us in the death and resurrection of the Lord Jesus Christ. We condemn ourselves for temptation and, like eating half a bag of potato chips, we think, "Well, I may as well eat the whole bag."

This emphasis disregards the place and position of the Holy Spirit in us. It turns us away from the presence of God in our lives, gets us totally self-absorbed, and leaves us in darkness, gasping in the air of this world rather than being powered by the atmosphere of heaven, the Spirit of God. We're meant to breathe, feed on, and live from the righteousness of Christ, Christ Himself inside us, every single moment.

Paul said, "Christ is all and in all" (Col. 3:11).

Jesus told us, "Nevertheless I tell you the truth. It is to your advantage that I go away; for if I do not go away, the Helper will not come to you; but if I depart, I will send Him to you" (John 16:7).

We're meant to breathe, feed on, and live from the righteousness of Christ, Christ Himself inside us, every single moment.

Major Ian Thomas wrote, "When you and I received Christ as our Redeemer, He gave us, through His Holy Spirit, the fullness and power of His resurrection. He has given us everything we could ever need at any time, under any circumstance. He gave us a car with a full tank; have you instead been trying to push it?

Whenever the gasoline is gone, it is not time for new upholstery, new spark plugs, or new tires; it is time to fill up the tank! Likewise, if our spiritual tank is empty, it is time to fill it. With what? With *Christ*."[1]

Our beliefs don't create reality, but the lies we hold in our heart eventually come into our attitudes and out through our actions. Biblical truth *is* reality, and it works out in us the same way.

Day 16

In Christ

For thus says the Lord God, the Holy One of Israel: "In returning and rest you shall be saved; in quietness and confidence shall be your strength." But you would not.

ISAIAH 30:15

One of our most essential questions is "Who am I?" As children we naturally look for it in our parents, later in our friends, in our relationships, in our spouses, in our art, in our university degrees, in our work, in our possessions. Other identity questions are, "Am I loved?" "Am I lovable?" and "Do I have what life requires of me?"

When our personal world comes crashing down in struggles, trials, and troubles, when our old ways of finding identity completely stop working, we often begin looking for identity in a new place—the Bible.

This is a valuable step, because the Bible isn't just a book of rules, like an owner's manual for a new car or laptop. It goes into much more detail than that, telling us who we are as reborn sons and daughters of God. In some ways, it's a schematic or blueprint. Rightly then, we study the Bible, looking deeply into our design, finding glittering gemstones. *Who am I, Lord?* And it is certainly right and good to be thrilled that God sees us in all these beautiful, positive ways. We then set about trying to change our thoughts, attitudes, and actions by trying to believe specific verses of Scripture with our intellect.

But the Bible isn't our source of life. Identity verses aren't our source. They *point* to our source. Everything the Bible says we have, everything it says we are, comes from being "in Christ." Our identity comes to us from Jesus Christ Himself.

The phrase "in Christ" occurs over and over in the New Testament. To take just a few instances in 1 and 2 Corinthians, Paul says we "are sanctified in Christ Jesus," we "have hope in Christ," God "always leads us in triumph in Christ," and we are "in Christ Jesus, who became for us wisdom from God—and righteousness and sanctification and redemption."[1]

And this: "Therefore, if anyone is in Christ, he is a new creation; old things have passed away; behold, all things have become new" (2 Cor. 5:17).

Our new identity is "in Christ." It isn't found by trying to behave a certain way, or trying to make ourselves hold certain attitudes, or even in believing in important doctrines.

Our identity springs forth from a *Person*. Jesus said, "Come to Me, all you who labor and are heavy laden, and I will give you rest. Take My yoke upon you and learn from Me, for I am gentle and lowly in heart, and you will find rest for your souls. For My yoke is easy and My burden is light" (Matt. 11:28–30).

When Jesus said, "Come to Me," He didn't mean solely, "Come to the Bible and read about Me." In fact, He told the Pharisees,

"You search the Scriptures, for in them you think you have eternal life; and these are they which testify of Me. But you are not willing to come to Me that you may have life" (John 5:39–40).

The Scriptures are there to point us to Jesus. Every time we read the Bible it's telling us to come to Jesus, right at that moment, to recognize Him as real and present, that we are in Him, and He is in us.

Though they studied the Scriptures diligently, many of the Pharisees in the Gospels wouldn't return and rest; they refused quietness and confidence (Isa. 30:15). Their identity was based on their own effort, their studies, their own works and reputations.

There is a way of searching the Scriptures that doesn't lead to life; it can fill us with head knowledge that puffs us up and doesn't lead to spiritual fruit (Gal. 5:22–23). It leads to big heads and shrunken hearts.

There is also a way of searching the Scriptures that leads to life; the Bible can prompt us to turn to Jesus every time we read.

Jesus meant exactly what He said: *Come to Me*. "In returning and rest you shall be saved; in quietness and confidence shall be your strength" (Isa. 30:15).

"Come to Me, all you who labor and are heavy laden, and I will give you rest" (Matt. 11:28).

As we come to Him and recognize we are in Christ, and He is in us *right now*, as we still all our soul-noise, Jesus brings quietness and confidence. The stillness in our soul and confidence in God will be the strength of our day, and as we continue to practice turning to Him, Christ will be the strength of our life. This is the practice of abiding dependence.

Day 17

Belief and Faith

"For God so loved the world that He gave His only begotten Son, that whoever believes in Him should not perish but have everlasting life. For God did not send His Son into the world to condemn the world, but that the world through Him might be saved."

JOHN 3:16–17

It is one of the loveliest thoughts in all of Scripture that God loves the world so much that He has given His all to save it. The hinge is "whoever believes in Him." "Whoever" simply means "anyone." It seems we need to look at that little word, "believe." What is it?

Our English word "believe" can mean "I intellectually agree with an idea." But Jesus and the New Testament writers often use a Greek verb meaning "to have faith in" or "to entrust."[1] And Jesus in John 3:16 uses the present tense, so it's more like, "Whoever is actively trusting in Him." This active trust, of course, still involves intellectual acceptance. But mere agreement in this sense is not entrusting, placing our confidence in God and His Son. It's only a mental nod. I can accept the *idea about* Jesus saving the world without placing any of my confidence in the fact.

Even natural, everyday faith isn't just intellectual assent. We live by natural faith, every day. I want to sit. I believe with my mind that the kitchen chair will hold me when I sit in it, but that belief by itself isn't faith. I must act on the belief to rest my feet, so I sit in the chair. The chair responds to my faith-action by holding me.

I want to fly to California, and I believe a big metal tube weighing hundreds of tons piloted by someone I don't know will get me to my destination. Faith brings action, and I buy a ticket and get on the plane. The plane and pilot I take by faith take me to California.

I desire and I believe what I desire is available. I choose faith, and I take—and then the thing takes me. I sit, I fly, I eat, I drive, I sleep by faith, by trust, by seeing something as reliable and taking it.

If someone won't do these ordinary things, if they're terrified of planes, or they carefully inspect every chair before they sit in it, we say they're abnormal, because to operate by faith in this way *is* normality. Most of us eat, drive, work, sleep, and live by this natural kind of faith, every single day of our lives.

Faith is action, based upon belief. These faith-choices are sustained by a growing sense of confidence. A child grows in these kinds of natural faith—faith to run, to ride a bike, to cook, to make friends.

Biblical faith has this same gut-level trust, but the object of this trust isn't a chair, a plane, or a pilot. We trust the invisible

God (Ex. 34:6), the God whose Spirit pours forth "love, joy, peace, patience, kindness, goodness, faithfulness, gentleness, and self-control" (Gal. 5:22–23 NET).

We can't drum up this trust through our minds, our willpower, or our emotions. We can learn God is trustworthy in part by what others say; we can learn about Him through the Bible, and of course to truly hear the written Word prompts faith to flow. But developing a stable, solid trust in God comes from being relational with Him, through fellowship, through sharing and partnering in His life. We still our souls, shut off our minds, turn off the chattering input from media and the noise and clatter of everyday life. We quiet ourselves, saying, "Bless the LORD, O my soul; and all that is within me, bless His holy name! Bless the LORD, O my soul, and forget not all His benefits" (Ps. 103:1–2). We still all the chatter and noise, sit quietly, and set our mind toward God, maybe focusing on a short passage of Scripture. Then we listen.

When I was younger, I thought to "have faith" in God meant trying to believe that His promises were true, exerting mental or emotional effort to convince myself. As I get older it seems to me that faith in God is much more about knowing Him personally and trusting *Him*—who He is, His character, His goodness—and less about only trying to believe His promises. Although it's crucial to trust in what God tells us, we need to remember the center of trust, of reliance, of rest, is trusting who God is—that He is good, and His love never fails. When *knowing God* is a daily experience, trusting in what He says is a lot easier.

Biblical faith is a gut-level reliance on the goodness of God, the kindness of God, the favor and love of God. It means we internally "bet the farm" on Him because we *know* Him. In every decision, in every circumstance, with every new situation, trial, or trouble, we begin to leap continually into the bottom line: *Abide, right now.* We keep the flow open and know God is present, God is good, God is kind, and God is doing absolutely everything He can to conform our lives into the image or reflection of Christ.

As with the chair or the plane, we desire God; we want Him to change our lives, and we see He's available and trustworthy. We take Him by faith and sit in His goodness, character, and promises; God then takes us and upholds us.

> *Biblical faith is a gut-level reliance on the goodness of God, the kindness of God, the favor and love of God. It means we internally "bet the farm" on Him because we know Him.*

God has an IQ infinitely beyond any known intelligence, and He holds an absolute, unshakable, ultimate, eternal love for us. It isn't any stretch to say that trusting Him is the smartest thing we can possibly do. Conversely, to not trust Him, instead trusting in our own limited IQ to figure life out, is the most foolish thing we can do. It's the difference between building a stone castle on bedrock or building on sand.

Foundations matter. When we build on the bedrock of recognizing God is with us, in us, all around us, in our circumstances, working all things together for good to those who love Him, we're building confidence in Him, and He works in us.

Day 18

Be Weak

For though He was crucified in weakness, yet He lives by
the power of God. For we also are weak in Him, but we
shall live with Him by the power of God toward you.

2 CORINTHIANS 13:4

We often spend a lot of time trying to become strong Christians. We study the Bible, go to church, and join accountability groups in the search for strength.

But the qualification for strength is weakness. "Come to Me, all you who labor and are heavy laden, and I will give you rest" (Matt. 11:28). The Greek word for "labor" means "to grow weary, tired, exhausted."[1] It means we've used up our strength.

A weak person is the only one asked to come to Jesus. Self-reliant, proud, independent people won't, like the Pharisees, Herod, and Pilate, because they don't see their need. Weak people have been broken down to recognize their weakness. For the most part, they've stopped living by their own willpower, effort, and trying to be "the little engine that could."

A weak person is the only one asked to come to Jesus. Self-reliant, proud, independent people won't, like the Pharisees, Herod, and Pilate, because they don't see their need.

God told the apostle Paul, "My grace is sufficient for you, for My strength is made perfect in weakness," and Paul goes on to say, "Therefore most gladly I will rather boast in my infirmities, that the power of Christ may rest upon me. Therefore I take pleasure in infirmities, in reproaches, in needs, in persecutions, in distresses, for Christ's sake. For when I am weak, then I am strong" (2 Cor. 12:9–10).

To find strength in every situation, we first recognize we're weak. We admit we don't have all the answers, the wisdom, or the strength we need.

If I'm strong, independent, and self-reliant, I'll be using my own human strength, intellect, and willpower to overcome tough situations. I'll be operating from my IQ, my upbringing, Bible knowledge, my own wisdom, and books I've read. There's nothing wrong with any of those things in themselves, but without recognizing the omnipresent God in ourselves and in the situation, we're walking in the dark. We can't see eternal issues. We "do the best we can." The book of Judges has a phrase for this: "In those days there was no king in Israel; everyone did what was right in his own eyes" (Judg. 17:6).

But Jesus said, "I am the vine; you are the branches. The one who remains in me—and I in him—bears much fruit, because apart from me you can accomplish nothing" (John 15:5 NET).

If we rely on the Holy Spirit in us, seeing Him as real, present, and powerful, we'll experience wisdom from the infinite God. Just as Jesus often said the unexpected thing, we'll begin to do the same. We'll be set apart by our reactions to situations. We'll begin to experience and express love, joy, peace, patience, and all the rest. We'll act in ways that people don't expect. God will enter and redeem situations and relationships that are broken.

If I see myself as "a strong Christian," I'm setting myself up for failure. We can see how well independence works in Romans 7. When we live there, God lets us. When we try to live life in our own strength and wisdom, God sits back and waits. When we work with frantic effort, God rests. If we pray for Him to bless our effort, He likely won't. He waits for us to get finished with our own ways, our own coping mechanisms, our own independence. He waits for us to recognize our weakness.

If I see myself as weak and I go to God recognizing I am finite, limited, and unable to see the whole situation as He does, I'm setting myself up to receive strength from the vine. In any situation, He will bring things into my mind and heart to say and do.

When we rest, relying on and trusting in God, He goes to work.

To clarify, rest is not passivity; it produces the opposite. Resting in Christ gives us a capability to do much more than working from our own strength. It's active. We sit, we quiet our soul-noise, and listen. We expect God to give us the wisdom we lack, the strength we need. These are all actions—inner actions. And taking this kind of inner action and making it a habit begins to transform our thoughts, attitudes, and outer actions.

When we rest, relying on and trusting in God, He goes to work.

Practicing guitar from a sense of confidence, ability, and sufficiency gives me a sense of trust and hope about improving and playing well. This gives me a more restful attitude and allows me to pay attention to my technique. I learn more quickly, and faster learning builds a sense of confidence, ability, and sufficiency. It's a positive, self-fulfilling loop. Confident faith makes me *more* active, not less, because I work from hope—the expectation of good things coming.

Which is more passive in a heated discussion—taking a breath or two to rest in Christ and recognize He is in you and in the other person, and then responding with love and patience, or reacting with fleshly effort to convince the other person you're right? Entering His rest, or a primal reaction?

Which is more passive—to live every day in fear, tension, and stress, letting our minds wander willy-nilly over every possible bad scenario, or to be continually "casting all your anxieties on him, because he cares for you" (1 Peter 5:7 ESV), and using our imaginations to think through possibilities? Tumbling in the flood of our natural reactions, or trusting God to be our strength to get us to the solidity of the riverbank?

Recognizing our weakness is the way to standing in His strength.

Day 19

Light and Seeing

This is the message which we have heard from Him
and declare to you, that God is light and
in Him is no darkness at all.

1 JOHN 1:5

J esus made many references to light: a light on a lampstand,
the light of a city on a hill. Light gives illumination to "those who
sit in darkness and the shadow of death, to guide our feet into the
way of peace." Light reveals what is hidden.[1]

If light lessens in a room, colors and details fade. As the darkness thickens, forms begin to vanish, and when the light is gone,
we see nothing. In total darkness, every view looks the same: up,
down, sides, front, back. Darkness obscures all difference, all color,
all detail, all beauty.

C. S. Lewis wrote, "How monotonously alike all the great tyrants and conquerors have been: how gloriously different are the
saints."[2]

Darkness obscures the beauty and God-created uniqueness of a human personality. An addict, a narcissist, or a thief have made a lifestyle of something dark. They've been deceived; in the beginning, drugs promised freedom from emotional pain; narcissism promised control over fear and gave a sense of sufficiency; stealing overcame the fear of lack.

In each case, the *desires* themselves aren't wrong. The desire for freedom from emotional bondage, the desire to feel in control, to avoid lack, or to feel important—these are all normal human desires.

When we try to reach to achieve good desires using the wrong means, habit lowers the light, blinds us, then binds us. The darkness closes in, and soon an occasional drug user is living and acting like addicts do, with thoughts, attitudes, and behaviors common to all addicts. The colors and details of personality fade as darkness fills the inner rooms of the soul. As George MacDonald wrote, "For all wickedness tends to destroy individuality, and declining natures assimilate as they sink."[3]

It's impossible to have one's mind and heart full of the pursuit of addiction, narcissism, and theft, or money and power, and at the same time be in continual fellowship with God. Jesus tells us the two things are mutually exclusive. And John says it even more comprehensively: "Whoever abides in Him does not sin" (1 John 3:6).

This isn't an issue of whether God loves us. It doesn't mean we never sin, or that we must "get saved" all over again when we do. Sin is a fellowship problem. We're turned in the wrong direction, trying to get our desires and needs met. As a son or daughter, we're ignoring the voice of our Father, thinking we know what we need better than He does.

Light drives out darkness. When I flip the light on, darkness is dispelled. Light and darkness don't coexist. Light overcomes the dark wherever it shines. There may be a few places the dark can hide—under the desk, behind the speakers, under the bookshelf. But if I shine a flashlight there, the darkness can't hide, and it can't fight the light; it immediately disappears, and hidden things are revealed—thick dust, a guitar pick, a lost screw. There's nothing the dark can do *against* the light. It can only melt away.

The apostle John tells us, "This is the message which we have heard from Him and declare to you, that God is light and in Him is no darkness at all. If we say that we have fellowship with Him, and walk in darkness, we lie and do not practice the truth. But if we walk in the light as He is in the light, we have fellowship with one another, and the blood of Jesus Christ His Son cleanses us from all sin" (1 John 1:5–7).

Day 20

Metanoia:
Children of Mercy

The LORD's mercies... are new every morning.

LAMENTATIONS 3:22-23

Every day is a new start.

The Latin word "repentance" carries the idea of "penance," or paying for one's sins. It holds a lot of baggage. I've often heard people talk about "a lifestyle of repentance," and they often seem to mean, "Recognize you're a terrible sinner, remember God loves you, try hard to be good, and someday you're going to heaven." We often attempt to pay for our sins and to become better by using negative self-talk, by trying harder, or by doing good things out of a sense of guilt.

The Greek word translated "repentance" is *metanoia*.[1] Subtracting the baggage, it simply means "to change your mind." The Hebrew word for "repent" means something like "turn" or "return" or "to convert."[2] It is a change of direction. *Change your mind, and return to God, that your errors, your mistakes, your sins may be obliterated, wiped away, erased.*

To walk with God is to go with Him in a direction. We can't walk with Him and gossip, or lie, or look at pornography, because God doesn't go that way. Going the wrong way begins with a thought coming through our head. At that moment, we choose to chew on the thought, which brings more thoughts. We've opened a Pandora's box. Our attitude changes, and our behavior darkens because we've turned from our face-to-face stance toward God, from trusting and following Him, hiking off His road in a wrong direction. Eventually the thorns, thick brush, ticks, and snakes drive us back onto the road with God.

Our *relationship* with God as sons and daughters is never in question; His aim is to keep the *fellowship* going steadily. He wants us to continually *know* we are loved and accepted, and further, that He lives in us as our internal strength, our power to be who we are meant to be, to become who He created us to become.

When I was a freshman in high school, I began walking into town during my lunch hour and stealing—a deck of cards, a candy bar, things like that. It was uncharacteristic of me; I was my mom's "good kid." I loved the library, played my guitar, and got good grades. I was obedient and helpful. But I'd watched older kids steal, and without thinking I fell into the same behavior.

I was an inept criminal; in just a few days I was caught stealing a Waylon & Willie cassette from a music store. The owner grabbed my arm, sat me down on the floor behind the counter, and called the police.

As I sat handcuffed in the police car, I can't tell you how terrified

I was; my mind was full of kids I knew who had gone to juvenile hall and even jail. At the station, the policeman asked me questions about my home life. After the paperwork was done, he told me to go back to school, ride the school bus home, and tell my mom what I'd done.

It was a miserable day. I couldn't stop thinking of how disappointed my mom would be. I finally got home and huddled up on the couch until she came home from work. Mom had had a hard life at times, and I was her "good kid" who never got in any trouble, so I was sick about what I'd done.

Mom stepped in and saw my distress. She asked with concern, "What's wrong?"

I blurted it out. "I got caught stealing today."

Silence. She was shocked and said in disbelief, "*You?*"

I said nothing and looked down, ashamed. She stared at me.

Then she said something I've never forgotten. She said, "Well—I know you'll never do it again."

That was it. She never brought it up again, and I never did it again. She went right back to trusting me that very moment.

That's what God's mercy looks like when He sees our *metanoia.*

The apostle Paul wrote, "Do not be conformed to this world, but be transformed by the renewing of your mind, that you may prove what is that good and acceptable and perfect will of God" (Rom. 12:2). An important point: we've got to stop the self-hating self-talk. I've said and done foolish things in my life, too, and until the early 1990s, I talked negatively about myself endlessly, even in my prayer journal. I thought I was practicing humility, but negative self-talk isn't humility; it's pride and self-obsession. God doesn't want this from us. He wants *metanoia,* that simple turning to recognize Him as real, present, and in us. He wants confession. Confession involves telling the truth, which means we say, "I did that, and it was wrong." It also means we agree with God, recognizing He doesn't determine our status with Him and our identity by how we behaved.

Self-hatred and negative self-talk are counterproductive; they cement us into the wrong mindset and chain us to wrong behaviors. We're bolstering the false identity and forgetting who we really are in Christ.

> *Self-hatred and negative self-talk are counterproductive; they cement us into the wrong mindset and chain us to wrong behaviors.*

If we *have* done wrong, we don't harden our hearts, make excuses, and stubbornly keep on in the wrong direction. We do an about-face back to fellowship, turning and looking directly at our Father again. His mercies are new, every time.

This is the daily life of turning face-to-face with God, putting the thoughts of His heart into our hearts and minds, those ways He thinks about us, about life, about reality. We sit quietly for a time, learning to clear our minds of thoughts, distractions, and today's tasks.

This is daily conversion, daily *metanoia*. It brings day-by-day transformation because it fills our hearts and minds with the Holy Spirit daily. We can't learn to do anything well—guitar, archery, cooking, painting—unless we do it regularly. Regular fellowship with God puts us in contact with *Life*. This doesn't necessarily mean hours and hours, though we can have those times of prayer, of course. This daily fellowship means we take moments throughout the day to remember and recognize who God is, where He is, and what He says about who we are. This is to "pray without ceasing" (1 Thess. 5:17), where life becomes a dialogue. We open ourselves up and move toward living in the awareness of our continual connection with Him.

Amy Carmichael, the Irish missionary to India, wrote, "Keep close, keep close. If you are close you will be keen. Your heart will be set on the things that abide. You will drink of His spirit and you will thirst for souls even as He thirsts. You will not be attracted by the world that crucified Him, but you will love the people in that world who have never seen His beauty and are losing so much more than they know. You will live to share your joy in Him. Nothing else will count for much."[3]

Day 21

Sunlight on the Dust: Sons and Daughters of God

> Because you are sons, God has sent forth the Spirit of His
> Son into your hearts, crying out, "Abba, Father!" There-
> fore you are no longer a slave but a son, and if a son, then
> an heir of God through Christ.
>
> GALATIANS 4:6-7

W hen we pray, "Our Father," we are to say the word with all the associations that the most loving, kind, perfect Father would bring, despite whatever kind of earthly father we may have.

A good father has children because he *wanted* them. He antic- ipates and provides for their needs, and usually gives them what they want if it isn't harmful in some way. Sometimes he withholds what they want because he has a better idea. He does what he says he'll do. He disciplines his kids in love; he straightens out their thinking, attitudes, words, and actions while minding their hearts. He isn't harsh, and he doesn't discourage his children.

A good father has his children's best interests at heart, even at the expense of his own. He wants them to be strong, fearless, loving, compassionate adults who contribute to the well-being of others.

When I spend time with God and see what this Father is really like, the first thing I notice is my own fathering, and how far it has sometimes been from this ideal.

It's probably this aspect of getting close with God that makes us stand at a slight distance from Him. We know close contact with Him will involve seeing our wrong attitudes and ways of doing things. It will involve change, and change is hard, so we think, "As long as I read my Bible, pray, go to church, and give, that's enough." Those are good things, but they're not necessarily the same as living in close fellowship with God. C. S. Lewis wrote as the demon Screwtape, "In avoiding this situation—this real nakedness of the soul in prayer—you will be helped by the fact that the humans themselves do not desire it as much as they suppose. There's such a thing as getting more than they bargained for!"[1]

So at times, as a dad, when even for a moment I truly see the perfectly loving Father, I've wanted to weep, because when the streaks of morning sun come through the window and reveal the floor, it's very easy to notice the dirt and cat hair on the wood, and the layer of dust all over everything, and to forget that there *is* a beautiful wood floor, that there are walls with good memories, a roof to keep out the rain, and furniture, and so much more to be grateful for.

In a month of parenting, or in any relationship, it's easy to focus on a few bad moments and forget thousands of moments of love, compassion, conversation, reading together, eating together, and joy.

But in my relationship with God, I'm sometimes the boy who didn't know better, the boy who was often trying to do the best he knew, but independently—the boy who needs to know he is loved, that his Father has his back, that he has the Spirit. I'm the kid whose seeing and thinking need adjustment so my future will go well.

What I don't need right then is condemnation. I don't need my own self-condemnation, and God doesn't ever give any (Rom. 8:1).

I don't need to fix anything right then, and the last thing I need to avoid is the deep look into the eyes of my Father.

> God will give words of correction, of adjustment. But they're never condemning words. His corrections speak to our actions, not to our identity as His children. Love and acceptance from our Father are part of our inheritance in Christ.

It's right to be sad over hurt we've caused, and it's always right to apologize to others where needed. But it's never right to hate and condemn ourselves. To condemn ourselves is adding sin on top of sin, because we're not believing in the cleansing blood of Jesus and the love and acceptance of our Father. Self-condemnation is self-righteousness dressed up in false humility. It's believing, "I ought to have been better" and being miserable at the failure of our self-effort.

When very few people were recognizing God as present and real and loving, Jesus prayed for them: "Father, forgive them, for they do not know what they do" (Luke 23:34). And we really, truly don't. We can see it only by the light streaming in the window.

Our deepest need from God at such times is for love, acceptance, the deep conviction that we are always sons and daughters, always cared for. If we stay in the abiding awareness of His presence, that's what He gives. God will give words of correction, of adjustment. But they're never condemning words. His corrections speak to our actions, not to our identity as His children. Love and acceptance from our Father are part of our inheritance in Christ.

So I keep most of my attention on the sunlight streaming through the window. It's a good thing when the light has shown me the floor needs a solid sweeping. I can get to that—after this time with my Father. In this moment, my time is better spent as His child. He's always guiding, teaching, and growing me up.

Day 22

A Father Addresses His Sons

And have you forgotten the exhortation addressed to you
as sons? "My son, do not scorn the Lord's discipline or give
up when he corrects you. For the Lord disciplines the one
he loves and chastises every son he accepts."

HEBREWS 12:5-6 NET

I have often forgotten this encouragement. God disciplines me
because I am a son, because He loves me, because He is growing
me up into the image of Christ. I've often held to the shreds of
my childhood view of God as a somewhat distant, annoyed father
concerned only with my "being good" rather than seeing God's
love in His discipline.

But discipline can *encourage* us, which means *to fill us with
courage.*

George MacDonald wrote, "One thing is clear in regard to every trouble—that the natural way with it is straight to the Father's

knee. The Father is father *for* his children, else why did he make himself their father?"[1]

Love manifests in any decent parent as expressed affection, encouragement, affirmation, giving, teaching, training, disciplining, and rebuking.

> How precious is Your lovingkindness, O God!
> Therefore the children of men put their trust under the shadow
> of Your wings. (Ps. 36:7)

But discipline can encourage us, which means to fill us with courage.

In the kingdom, we're God's spiritual children—we start as spiritual babies, then toddlers, taking our first steps, His kindergarteners, entering life's school. We're His grade schoolers, middle schoolers, high schoolers. We're His sons and daughters entering college, entering life, finally becoming full grown, embracing the responsibilities and privileges of being grown-up. These are necessary stages in our spiritual lives.

We can't mature if we're never trained, disciplined, or rebuked.

"Before I formed you in the womb I knew you" (Jer. 1:5). We were planned, birthed with intent, and here is God's ultimate purpose:

> Till we all come to the unity of the faith and of the knowledge
> of the Son of God, to a perfect man, to the measure of the
> stature of the fullness of Christ; that we should no longer be
> children, tossed to and fro and carried about with every wind
> of doctrine, by the trickery of men, in the cunning craftiness of
> deceitful plotting, but, speaking the truth in love, may grow up

in all things into Him who is the head—Christ—from whom the whole body, joined and knit together by what every joint supplies, according to the effective working by which every part does its share, causes growth of the body for the edifying of itself in love. (Eph. 4:13–16)

The Father's intent is to create a vast family of mature, grown-up sons and daughters who live in Him, seeing with His eyes, loving with His love, walking in willing cooperation with God and others, no longer being childish in the sense of following every thought, whim, feeling, or inclination that happens to pass by.

God's love, affection, and character cannot be less than that of a human being. He cannot love one whit less than the best mother. He cannot dwell on the future of His children any less than the best human father.

As God, He's *infinitely more;* He loves more, cares more, plans more, and disciplines more. He trains us because He has a future for us. He corrects us because we are sons and daughters. He never gets tired and never gives up. He disciplines because He loves us with eternal love.

He knew us before we were born. He *planned* us. We are His poem, His artwork, His craftsmanship, His new creation—His sons and daughters (Ps. 40:5; Jer. 29:11; Eph. 2:10).

If there is a God who loves us like that, a Father who loves us with a love *deeper* than the love we have for our own sons and daughters, then we're safe in that love, safe in His discipline, safe even in His rebuking. He wants the absolute best for us. No matter what happens in our lives, we have a refuge. I want *that* God, in Christ, to live in me, through me, as the source and ground of my life. I want the forever-loving Father to say, "This is my beloved son, in whom I am well pleased." That takes training, discipline, and sometimes a rebuke. I want Christ in me to say, "Abba, Father" every day and embrace it all.

Day 23

Named and Blessed

Blessed be the God and Father of our Lord Jesus Christ,
who has blessed us with every spiritual blessing in the
heavenly places in Christ, just as He chose us in Him before the foundation of the world, that we should be holy
and without blame before Him in love, having predes-
tined us to adoption as sons by Jesus Christ to Himself,
according to the good pleasure of His will, to the praise
of the glory of His grace, by which He made us accepted
in the Beloved.

EPHESIANS 1:3–6

At this very moment we're blessed with *every* spiritual blessing. Our Father chose us to be His children and has accepted us
in the Beloved, in Christ.

"For this reason I bow my knees to the Father of our Lord
Jesus Christ, from whom the whole family in heaven and earth
is named" (Eph. 3:14–15). We're not only blessed; we're named.
We have a God-given identity.

But we often have false concepts of who we are. As children

born into this fallen world, we take the world's names to heart. People say and do negative things toward us, whether intentionally or (more often) unintentionally, and those negatives are based on how they see us. But how people see us is often colored by how they see themselves. We're born without a sense of identity, and for much of our lives we depend on people with broken, distorted ideas of their own identity to tell us who we are.

Without knowing what we're doing, we take these false names into ourselves. We do this especially as children, often naming ourselves for the rest of our lives. Then, like those who named us, we propagate our way of thinking to others—most often unintentionally.

Jesus prayed, "Forgive them, Father. They don't know what they are doing." The bully in the schoolyard pushes other kids around and tells them they're stupid and weak. Yes, he needs to be stopped. But what do you suppose the bully has going on at home?

Even people who intentionally spread misery are to some degree following their earthly programming, utterly deceived about what life is about. It's one reason why Jesus went to the cross—to reset us, to rename us, to give us a new birth, a new life, a new start.

We don't have to live from these false identities that have been handed down to us, imposed on us by the names we have been called, the names we have fed ourselves on for years. George MacDonald wrote, "There is no forgetting of ourselves but in the finding of our deeper, our true self—God's idea of us when he devised us—the Christ in us."[1]

We have a Father who has chosen us and named us with eternal names; He knows our real selves. He chose us before the world was made, before we were born, before anyone made us feel the negatives *unwanted, stupid, lazy, bad, clumsy, untalented,* or *unloved.* Or the positives: *The good one. The responsible one. The smart one. The favorite.* There may be elements of truth in these. Even positive names can set us up for a lifetime of trying to prove ourselves, of feeling overly responsible, of perfectionism, and even worse, they can birth in us a deeply rooted feeling of self-satisfaction and pride.

God's names are true reality. He favors us, even when we're lost and wandering, "dead in sins and trespasses," and He takes us to Himself and tells us the names He gave us. We don't make a name for ourselves. So remember who you really are.

You are blessed with every spiritual blessing. Peter puts it this way: "His divine power has given to us all things that pertain to life and godliness, through the knowledge of Him who called us by glory and virtue" (2 Peter 1:3). In Christ, you are blessed with everything you need today, right now, for life and godliness—as surely as God is present with you and in you.

According to Ephesians 1:3–6, a few of your names are:

Sons and daughters of God. Children of an eternal Father. You can begin to stop thinking and behaving like an orphan. The Father is here, with you.

Chosen. You were wanted, *desired.* It means you can begin to turn away from the lies that say otherwise.

Accepted in the Beloved. You are acceptable and accepted in Christ. You are in Him, and Christ is in you.

Peter goes on to say, "By which have been given to us exceedingly great and precious promises, that through these you may be partakers of the divine nature, having escaped the corruption that is in the world through lust" (2 Peter 1:4).

Partaker of the divine nature. It means we feed and sustain our lives on God—His love for us, His care for us, His names for us. It means *we've been given the same nature as God*—His Spirit in us. Gifted, blessed, son of God, daughter of God, chosen, accepted in the Beloved, partaker of the divine nature—you are one who has everything you need for life and godliness, today, right this moment.

Yet our choice remains. We take a willed share in our own making. Will I trust God, or will I trust anything and everything else? The prodigal didn't trust his father because he didn't know his father's heart, and neither did the elder brother. To know God well involves being with Him and hearing His heart. To know any person, to trust them and what they say, is something grown. As we grow in *knowing* we're loved, kept, watched over, filled full, blessed, and partakers of God's nature, this *knowing* will begin to spill out into our actions.

You are one who has everything you need for life and godliness, today, right this moment. Yet our choice remains. We take a willed share in our own making.

So we take God's words on our true identity to heart; it's not just dead information pinned to a card. His words are Spirit—relational, and alive, and transformative—that is, it changes how we see God, ourselves, and others, and those inner changes grow out into how we act.

Day 24

God the Giver

We love Him because He first loved us.

1 JOHN 4:19

When I was younger, I used to think I was a good musician because I'd worked hard. I did spend a lot of time in focused practice, and still do. But with age, I've realized how my circumstances and those around me helped shape me into the musician that I am. My dad owned a music store full of instruments; he and my stepmom gave me my first guitar, banjo, bluegrass albums, instructional books, and lessons. They loaned me about six thousand dollars for my first car and provided me with a job at the store to pay it off. My family ingrained a strong work ethic in me from a young age. I was suddenly mobile and able to drive myself to bluegrass festivals, connecting with other players and honing my craft. Everything blossomed from there.

So, I didn't *earn* my accomplishments solely by my own hard work. I had a lot given to me early on that prepared me. I still practice, but my practice is a response to what I've been given.

We're not often trained to think this way. We're trained in the "earn it" mindset from very early on, and we can easily carry that attitude with us when we come into the kingdom of God. The way of the kingdom is the opposite. God gives, we receive, and then we use, enjoy, and expand what we've received.

Paul says to the Corinthians, "What do you have that you did not receive?" (1 Cor. 4:7).

In the kingdom—this kingdom Jesus said is here with us right now—we get everything before we do anything. Everything we need is given to us as a bag of seeds, and we're to plant, water, cultivate, grow, and expand the seeds by relying on God; we recognize what we've been given, we take it, and in trust and reliance we step out to expand it (see Matt. 25:14–30).

So, at the same time, if I hadn't given myself wholeheartedly to learning and growing my musical skills, I wouldn't be playing music for a living today. My decades-long career in music has come from a God-given desire and the resources and generosity of the family I was planted in, combined with my response to all that I have been given.

God first gives, and then we respond. Paul asked the Galatians, "Did you receive the Spirit by works of the law or by hearing with faith?" (Gal. 3:2 ESV). We didn't do anything to earn God's love, God's Spirit, His favor, His peace. He gives it because it is His nature to love and to give.

God loves you and is utterly devoted to you. The apostle John told us, "God is love" (1 John 4:8). The Greek word there for "love" is *agape.*[1] It means He is wholeheartedly committed to your present, future, and eternal well-being. His love came to you—first. It never, ever goes away. And this love is not a *thing* God has; it pours out of His very being. He *is* love.

Now, think about this with me for a moment. If you spend quality time with an exceedingly wise, loving friend who cares about who you are, cares about your character, listens to you, and counsels you from wisdom whenever you ask, whose very being is alive with love for you, do you ever have to strive or try to love, trust, respect, or cherish them? Is it a big effort to be thankful or grateful, or to tell others about how amazing this person is? Is it hard, if you trust someone, to take their advice and do as they say? Is it hard to spend time with them?

All rhetorical questions. To return real love isn't an effort; it's a *reflexive response.*

By "quality time" with God, I don't necessarily mean Bible study, reading a devotional, journaling, or any other form of "doing." It's possible to do those things solely with the *mind.* Quality time with God may or may not involve those things. There is no *rule* here.

In quality time, we might sit quietly, thanking Him for His presence with us, in us, letting the *awareness* and *recognition* of His presence fill our minds and hearts for a time. It means shutting off the mind for part of our time to everything but sitting alone with God as we really see and know His presence inside us and around us. Bible study, journaling, and all that are done with this awareness.

For Jesus, Paul, and John, the underlying root of our lives is this: "God loves you before you have ever done anything."

Our love, *agape,* our wholehearted commitment-love toward

God, is a reflexive response to God loving us. His love came first. His powerful Holy Spirit was given to us first. His life and resources have been put inside us first before any of our doing.

We won't *experience* God's love for us, His Spirit, His resources, if we never turn to look at Him or recognize Him as present. When we do, He'll begin to change the way we think, like any good father. Children behave better when they spend quality time with their father, which often involves just being together—reading, driving, and listening to music together, talking at the table, or other forms of *communing* with one another. As they commune with their father, they feel safe in his presence; they learn to trust him, to rely on him, and they begin to feel truly secure in their relationship with him, sheltered in his love. In this fellowship, God gives, we receive, and in His presence we feel confident to step out and expand what He gives.

Day 25

Believing Is Seeing

"Blessed are those who have not seen
and yet have believed."

JOHN 20:29

Much of the world operates on the maxim "Seeing is believing." When the disciples told Thomas after the crucifixion of Jesus that they'd seen Him alive, he responded the same way: "Unless I see ... I will not believe" (John 20:25).

But believing is true seeing. Every high-level painter, illustrator, musician, vocalist, author, cook, businessman, or songwriter has followed a process. They first desired and loved; they believed; they expected good things to come, and these ways of *being* gave energy to do years of work in patient endurance. Imagination is a big part of any creative process.

In the kingdom of God we have a deeper basis than the motto "Believe in yourself," because the wholehearted commitment-love of God is poured out into our hearts by the Holy Spirit (Rom. 5:5).

We've been given a divine download and made partakers of the divine nature through the magnificent and precious promises of God (2 Peter 1:4). Because God lives in us, we *desire* to be more loving, to have joy, peace, patience, gentleness, goodness, humility, faith, and self-control.

The second component, after desire, is to trust and rely on God wholeheartedly.

Let's talk about "believing" again for a moment. Our English word "believe" and the phrase "have faith" don't really do justice to the Greek word used in the New Testament. Belief can be "intellectual assent." "Having faith" sounds potentially passive; I can *have* a car and not drive it. Biblical faith—gut-level reliance on God's love, character, and power—goes much deeper.

The Hebrews following Moses desired the promised land, but that entire first generation died without it in the wilderness. They wanted what God promised, but they did not wholeheartedly entrust themselves to the God through whom it was possible. Instead of imagining how the promises of God would look when fulfilled, they used their imaginations to remember how "good" life had been in Egypt, how there was plenty to eat—forgetting the slavery and long, sweaty days of brickmaking. In their minds, attaining the land was impossible.

If they'd moved forward into the land of promise, freely entrusting themselves to the care, providence, power, and love of God, they could have been free to imagine, free to create new lives, free to rely on a God who took care of them. That can't be done without giving fears and anxieties to God and taking fullness and sufficiency from His hands.

To entrust ourselves wholeheartedly means we know God

and see Him as real, as present, as watching over us, as caring.
Trust means to release anxiety, to let go
of fears holding us back, because *we have
God*. It means reliance, so we seek refuge and flee to Him for protection;[1] it
means to cast our burdens onto the Lord.
Wholehearted trust means betting the
farm, imagining the promises of God as
true, real, and solid rather than letting the
enemy use our imaginations to neutralize
and paralyze us. Confidence.

> *To entrust ourselves wholeheartedly means we know God and see Him as real, as present, as watching over us, as caring.*

> Therefore, since a promise remains of entering His rest, let us
> fear lest any of you seem to have come short of it. For indeed the
> gospel was preached to us as well as to them; but the word which
> they heard did not profit them, not being mixed with faith in
> those who heard it. (Heb. 4:1–2)

If we're going to fear anything, let's fear not entering God's rest,
of not mixing the Word with this reliant trust that steps out in
action. God has set us up for growth. We're reborn as sons and
daughters, filled with God in Christ, and empowered to kill our
giants as we follow Jesus.

Day 26

Come to Me

"You search the Scriptures, for in them you think you
have eternal life; and these are they which testify of Me.
But you are not willing to come to Me
that you may have life."

JOHN 5:39-40

I've often noticed how easy it is to accept *ideas* from Scripture;
we often think intellectual acceptance of an idea is the same as
actively relying upon the God of those ideas.

If we read an extensive biography of Winston Churchill, we'd
learn of his history and accomplishment; how he thought, how
he felt, and how he responded in certain situations. We could
become experts, expounding to others his various doctrines and
deeds.

But for all our knowing *about* Churchill, we still wouldn't *know*
him.

We often treat Scripture as students learning a subject. We pick up the Bible as *God's Autobiography* or an owner's manual and read it, studying various ideas and doctrines about Him, drawing charts and graphs, making theories about how God thinks and why He does what He does, and we look for commandments to *do*.

Bible study and good doctrine are important. I've been diving into the Bible for much of my life, and I've not yet gotten to the bottom of it. It is foolish to be a Christian without reading and studying what the Bible says.

But knowing *about* God differs from *knowing* God and His ways. Knowing about a subject is necessary. Studying about music is a lifelong pursuit for me, but it offers no benefit unless I am also putting my fingers to strings, experiencing a relationship with the guitar daily. In practicing, I encounter obstacles and must continually *trust* I can overcome them to become a better musician. If I only read about guitars and guitar players, my head would be filled with a lot of erroneous ideas about what guitar life is like.

Knowing *about* God is important but it's an incomplete, grainy picture without living in daily fellowship with Him.

Studying the Bible, theology, or reading biographies of people like Hudson Taylor or Spurgeon can even be used to avoid direct contact with God, just as I can avoid practicing guitar by spending all my time watching videos of great guitarists. It's a vicarious thrill—unless we put the things we learn into practice.

Knowing about God is important but it's an incomplete, grainy picture without living in daily fellowship with Him.

The Bible does differ from ordinary books; it's a supernatural revelation. It can't be fully understood without relationship with the Holy Spirit. The Bible is meant to draw us ever more deeply into that living fellowship where we *pray without ceasing,* where we walk through our day with the full awareness God is with us, in us, for us, and through us—a lifestyle of abiding in Christ. It means we are never left solely to our own limited resources.

Knowing about God without actively recognizing His presence daily keeps us locked into several fruitless ways of life: we may look for "God's requirements" and then exhaust ourselves trying to do them. Or we may compare ourselves to "the bad people," rationalizing that we're not so bad. Or we may give in completely to relativistic hedonism and say, "I may as well enjoy doing whatever I feel, since 'Jesus paid it all' and I'm forgiven and I'm going to heaven when I die."

The ordinances of the tabernacle and temple in the centuries before Jesus taught people to approach God by a *system.* That system was right for that time—the old covenant. The temple had a giant, heavy curtain hiding the Most Holy Place where the high priest met with God on behalf of the people. He had to dress in special clothing, undergo purification rites, and do everything else properly before going into the presence of God on the Day of Atonement. If he didn't do all this properly, he might die when he went into God's presence.

When Jesus died after saying *tetelestai,* "It is finished" (John 19:30), that heavy curtain blocking the sight and sound of God was ripped from top to bottom (Matt. 27:51). It was a divine message; access was now wide open. The writer of Hebrews says, "Let us therefore come boldly to the throne of grace, that we may obtain mercy and find grace to help in time of need" (Heb. 4:16).

Our High Priest, Jesus, has already gone into the Most Holy

Place ahead of us, and He's torn that heavy curtain blocking our access to God like a sheet of paper, from top to bottom. He sits there on His throne at the right hand of the Father and says, "Come to Me."

According to Jesus, there's only one source of life, and it's not "Come to the Bible" or "Come to sermons" or "Come to more giving, more praying, more doing for Jesus." Not even "Come to your devotional."

Jesus says, "Come to Me."

Day 27

Children
of the Father

Behold what manner of love the Father has bestowed on
us, that we should be called children of God!

1 JOHN 3:1

God is Father. *Our* Father. For many, the image of God as a
loving, kind, present, wise, listening Father was stolen away at an
early age by emotionally distant, absent, or even abusive fathers
or mothers. Many have had parents who loved us but were overly
permissive or passive, or overly strict and punitive. For a child,
the actions of a parent or other trusted authority figures become
an underlay of subconscious biases toward God, the basis of any
thoughts of who God is and how God relates to us. Parents color
our conception of God.

When Jesus said to pray, "Our Father," He meant something
beyond the most perfect idea of a human father imaginable; He

meant God is the ideal, perfectly loving Father. And He is *ours*.

If we hold on to how our earthly father acted and see God with that lens, we won't see and experience the real, true God; we'll experience God colored with the god of our imagining, that passive, permissive, distant, absent, or abusive parent in our own mind.

If I am suspicious of someone, if I think they dislike me or even that they "have it in for me," it is likely that I will fit all their actions into the little box of my presuppositions. We often create our own experience of reality; our thoughts and attitudes toward people or situations will often determine the quality of our experience. Friendships cool, families argue incessantly, and marriages often fail on this one principle. And a relationship with God often never begins or remains merely intellectual because of how a person sees God.

God tells us to take all that negative thinking about "father" that came from early authority figures and throw it away, and yes, sometimes we need help from our close, wise friends, relatives, or a counselor to do that.

> But God, who is rich in mercy, because of His great love with which He loved us, even when we were dead in trespasses, made us alive together with Christ (by grace you have been saved), and raised us up together, and made us sit together in the heavenly places in Christ Jesus, that in the ages to come He might show the exceeding riches of His grace in His kindness toward us in Christ Jesus. (Eph. 2:4–7)

This Father has an unlimited bank account of mercy, kindness, and goodwill toward us. He has an ever-flowing river of living water coming from within Himself, a wholehearted commitment-love with which He loves us.

George MacDonald wrote, "The wise and prudent must make a system and arrange things to his mind before he can say, *I believe. The child sees, believes, obeys.*"[1]

"Professing to be wise, they became fools" (Rom. 1:22). The foolish child "sees through" his loving parents who want the best for him; he paints all their words and actions with his own paintbrush: "They're just trying to control me." This one thought will cloud all his thoughts and attitudes toward them and will cause him to make foolish choices. He won't think about the sound, loving advice based on their years of life experience because he won't see their words in the light of their love.

We're often so afraid of being deceived that we can't be taken out of the lies we're believing. John writes, "But as many as received Him, to them He gave the right to become children of God" (John 1:12).

We have a divinely given *right* to our perfect, loving Father.

As His beloved, cherished children, our part is to trust Him as the perfectly loving Father and obey Him as one who forever has our best interests at heart. In the same sermon, MacDonald continued, "When my being is consciously . . . in the hands of him who called it to live and think and suffer and be glad—given back to him by a perfect obedience—I thenceforward breathe the breath, share the life of God himself. Then I am free, in that I am true—which means one with the Father . . . Christ then is the Lord of life; his life is the light of men; the light mirrored in them changes them into the image of him, the Truth; and thus the truth, who is the Son, makes them free."[2]

Day 28

Fear Not

*"Therefore I tell you, do not worry about your life,
what you will eat or drink, or about your body,
what you will wear. Isn't there more to life than
food and more to the body than clothing?"*

MATTHEW 6:25 NET

The Bible uses the phrases "Do not fear," "Do not be afraid,"
and "Do not worry" over one hundred times. Jesus combines "Do
not fear" with the encouragement to "Be of good cheer," to have
courage, several times in the Gospels.

Fear generates thoughts, attitudes, and actions, and will cause
us to act in ways that are counterproductive. We can't serve God
and money at the same time; that is, we can't be terrified of lack,
or worshiping the self-sufficiency that money can create in us, yet
be living from the fullness of God in us. We can't serve the god
Fear and the real God at the same time; they're mutually exclusive (see Matt. 6:22–23).

Fear-based decision-making generates bad decisions. It's true financially, in parenting, in marriage, in work. It often happens that Christian parents who were a bit wild when they were teens hold a lot of fear for their own children. Their desire is to keep their kids safe—a right and good motive. But in acting from fear, they over-control; they try to be their children's saviors.

Rather than teaching their kids *how* to think and do, they try to teach them *what* to think and do. In the process, they transmit fear-messages throughout childhood, subtle or unsubtle, that say to the child, "You are bad, and you need me to make your decisions for you; you need me to tell you what to think and do, because otherwise you are going to go off the rails." This message often comes to fruition when teens go away to college, with no adult controlling their behavior. Since they believe "I am bad," they act that way. With no drill sergeant telling them what to do, with no capacity for courage-based thinking, they think they need their friends to tell them what to do.

This kingdom has been built on fear.

When Jesus told the disciples that they'd be arrested and stand before councils and beaten in the synagogues, He said, "Do not worry beforehand, or premeditate what you will speak. But whatever is given you in that hour, speak that; for it is not you who speak, but the Holy Spirit" (Mark 13:11).

The message of fear says, "I need to eat. I need clothing. I need shelter. I need to stay alive in this situation." Those are valid needs. And the *feeling* of fear isn't evil; it's simply human. But in letting it rule us and seeing ourselves as our own saviors from our fears, we live according to fear and make fear-based decisions.

The message of Jesus, of Paul, of the Lord to Joshua, to Moses, to Abraham, to David—the message of the Bible—is, "Be of good cheer! It is I; do not be afraid" (Matt. 14:27). The Greek word for "cheer" means *courage*.[1] Knowing Jesus is present brings courage, confidence, and comfort.

We have a God who is "The LORD our righteousness" (Jer. 23:6). Paul said his message was to preach "Christ in you, the hope of glory" (Col. 1:27). Is this indwelling, righteous God in us incapable of overcoming our besetting sins? Will we indulge fear of sin, consider ourselves our own saviors, and set out to establish our own righteousness by our human effort? Or will we trust the righteous God inside us, think situations through with Him, and act based on reliance on His righteousness in us, His strength and power in us?

Will we trust the righteous God inside us, think situations through with Him, and act based on reliance on His righteousness in us, His strength and power in us?

Fear of sin causes obsession with it. Our thoughts center on it, fear drives us, and we use every possible human way to avoid sin while simultaneously being obsessed with it. There is no time to think of God, His love for us, His strength in us. Paul prayed for the Ephesians, that "the eyes of your understanding [be] enlightened; that you may know what is the hope of His calling, what are the riches of the glory of His inheritance in the saints, and what is the exceeding greatness of His power toward us who believe, according to the working of His mighty power" (Eph 1:18–19).

God's mighty power is in us. We can stare into the face of our fears with Him. We can trust Him. *Do not be afraid: be of good courage.*

Day 29

My Peace

"Peace I leave with you, My peace I give to you;
not as the world gives do I give to you. Let not your heart
be troubled, neither let it be afraid."

JOHN 14:27

We often think of peace as something based on our circumstances. We say, "Can't I have a little peace around here for a moment?" But peace is something God has bestowed upon us. It is a gift.

That brings a question: Why do we feel anxiety so frequently? I don't mean clinical anxiety, paranoia, or anything like that. A good, believing therapist is often necessary to help us cut through the jungle of misconceptions that can grow in our minds from trauma, to connect us more deeply to who God is and who we are. But here I mean our ordinary anxieties about our work, our kids, our marriages, about everyday life, and the kinds of things that keep us up in the night.

Like a dull pain in the shoulder or a toothache, anxiety is a symptom—a symptom of leftover ways of thinking and being.

"Be anxious for nothing, but in everything by prayer and supplication, with thanksgiving, let your requests be made known to God; and the peace of God, which surpasses all understanding, will guard your hearts and minds through Christ Jesus" (Phil. 4:6–7).

Both Jesus and Paul tell us it is possible to have peace in bad circumstances. Jesus said, "My peace I give to you" to His disciples the night Judas betrayed Him, and later that same night their brother Peter betrayed Jesus three times. The very next day the disciples lived through the horrific crucifixion of their leader, a death designed by the Romans to inflict elongated suffering on the crucified and deal out the maximum fear, shame, and judgment to anyone considering the same path as the convict.

"Be anxious for nothing."

Now, to be clear, the disciples *did* feel all those things in those next few days. The real source of peace had not been given to them yet. Just before Jesus said, "My peace I give to you," He told them, "But the Helper, the Holy Spirit, whom the Father will send in My name, He will teach you all things, and bring to your remembrance all things that I said to you" (John 14:26).

What is anxiety? Again, I don't mean clinical anxiety or depression or any of that. I mean the ordinary fears and anxieties of being human, anxieties about failing, about not being liked or loved, about finances, about anything.

Anxiety is the result of holding certain beliefs deep down in the heart. "I am alone in this world and have to make my own way." "No one really likes me." "I am a failure." "Our family has always been poor, and we will always be poor." In such a case, it doesn't really matter if we later achieve a lot of friends, money, or success. We'll have anxieties about losing it all.

It's often called the orphan or poverty mindset, but it has little to do with money. It's the acceptance that God has given us only piddly, inadequate, insubstantial inner resources, and now we are forced to limp along forever until we die.

To go a little deeper, these anxieties we've held in the heart for so long come down to this: *I am an independent me, alone, trying to get through life by my own will and effort, and I don't have enough inner or outer resources to meet the need.*

To believe this is to believe and live from a lie. Our starting point is wrong, our aim is off, and this will necessarily make a lot of our thoughts, attitudes, and actions "miss the mark."

None of us is alone, not ever, not for a single moment. If God is omnipresent, as Christianity affirms, then He is everywhere at all times. This means He is right here, sitting with us, in the room with us, all around us—and inside us. Every one of us is capable of growth, of expansion, of walking into maturity and living from fullness and expectant hope. We aren't alone. We don't "make our own way in this world." We are deeply loved and liked, destined to be victorious at loving God and others because the source of love lives inside us.

Jesus said, "Let not your heart by troubled, neither let it be afraid" (John 14:27). He knew we had a choice to *let* or *let not*, that there is a door every day between two different lives. We can stay outside the door, allowing our hearts to be troubled and afraid. Or we can push through and enter the door, refusing anxiety and fear, embracing peace and rest.

That door is daily fellowship with God, recognition of God as real, present, and in us. "Let us therefore come boldly to the throne of grace, that we may obtain mercy and find grace to help in time of need" (Heb. 4:16).

Anxieties and fears will continue to flood into a heart any day we're holding that throne-room door shut from the wrong side. When we ruminate on anxieties and fears, allowing the flood, refusing to go in, we'll make bad decisions. And of course, since we were raised in this world, with its performance-based acceptance, its rules, its ways, our default habit is to figure things out for ourselves.

The kind of faith-life I'm talking about is something built, like a house, and it's built on the rock of God's unchanging goodness, love, and grace. It's built on going through those doors on a continual basis.

It's built on a continually flowing supply of peace we can embrace.

Day 30

Electricity

Christ the power of God.

1 CORINTHIANS 1:24

For by grace you have been saved through faith, and that
not of yourselves; it is the gift of God, not of works, lest
anyone should boast.

EPHESIANS 2:8-9

Our English word "grace" is from the Greek word *charis*,[1] from which we get *charisma*. This grace isn't merely "unmerited favor." Luke 2:52 says Jesus kept increasing in wisdom, stature, and *charis*. *Strong's Concordance* says *charis* is used of "the merciful kindness by which God, exerting his holy influence upon souls, turns them to Christ, keeps, strengthens, increases them in Christian faith, knowledge, affection, and kindles them to the exercise of the Christian virtues."[2]

Grace is God's favor and power, strengthening, influencing,

and powering up a human being. For us it *is* unmerited, a gift from God through the Lord Jesus Christ.

When I walk into the kitchen in the dark of an early morning, I flip on the light switch. Where does the electricity come from? Do I have to generate it? What happens to the dark when I flip on the switch? Where does it go?

Paul said his ministry was to make the riches of the glowing, luminescent mystery known among the Gentiles—the *revealed* mystery, hidden from generations: "Christ in you, the hope of glory" (Col. 1:27). He wanted them to know the source of love, favor, and power. He goes on to say, "Him we proclaim, warning everyone and teaching everyone with all wisdom, that we may present everyone mature in Christ" (Col. 1:28 ESV).

If we asked Paul, "*Why* did you go through all that? Why did you put up with all the opposition, hatred, beatings, all of it?" he would say his "why" was to preach "Christ in you, the hope of glory" and to show or present or prove every person as complete and whole in Christ. This was Paul's desire, his aim, his "why," because Jesus Christ had changed his life. Paul wanted to turn on the power and lights for all of us.

He finishes the first chapter of Colossians with this: "To this end I also labor, striving according to His working which works in me mightily" (Col. 1:29).

If we asked him, "*How* did you stand it? *How* did you deal with all the opposition, the hatred, being hunted, thrown in prison, whipped, being shipwrecked, and in continual danger of death?" his answer is Colossians 1:29. Paul said he agonized like an Olympic athlete with all the energy of God which was energizing him with dynamic power.

That was Paul's *how*. His job was to flip the switch and use the power. He didn't generate or sustain that power. He says in Galatians, "I am crucified with Christ: nevertheless I live; yet not I, but Christ liveth in me: and the life which I now live in the flesh I live by the faith of the Son of God, who loved me, and gave himself for me. I do not frustrate the grace of God: for if righteousness come by the law, then Christ is dead in vain" (Gal. 2:20–21 KJV).

In thinking we must create or sustain this energizing, grace-power of goodness, we frustrate or make void the power of the grace of God. Paul is saying, *If this righteousness-power can come by our own striving and trying to be good, then Christ died for nothing.*

Trying hard to be good by our own power is like walking into a dark room and lighting a little wooden match. It keeps us from reaching for the light switch.

Our little box of matches—the coping mechanisms, ways of manipulating people or situations, or whatever it is—that little box of temporary fixes will always *frustrate, reject, annul,* and *set aside* the grace-energy of God, because we are too busy finding our own solutions and listening to our own voice. That little match will burn out or blow out every time, and we'll end up sitting in the dark with ashes and burnt fingers.

God speaks through the prophet Isaiah,

> "Look, all you who kindle a fire,
> Who encircle yourselves with sparks:
> Walk in the light of your fire and in the sparks you have kindled—
> This you shall have from My hand:
> You shall lie down in torment." (Isa. 50:11)

When we live by our own way, our own means, our own coping mechanisms, we get nothing from God. The torment is self-generated. God lets our matches do what matches do. They give temporary, bad light, burn our fingers, and burn out, producing darkness and torment. Sometimes they burn the house down.

Trying hard to be good by our own power is like walking into a dark room and lighting a little wooden match. It keeps us from reaching for the light switch.

We don't have to try to beat back the darkness with matches or figure out how the power works. We flip the switch and walk in the light. The switch is *fellowship with God.* We thank God for His presence with us, for us, in each of us, and then we ask and *expect* Him to come through us.

When we are tempted, when darkness hits us, when we fail, we flip on the switch again, and again, and again. "Thank You, Lord, that You are present in the darkness, that You never leave or forsake me even when I sin. Thank You, Lord, that You redeem my past, are with me and in me in my present, and are taking care of my future. Thank You that in Christ, with Christ in me, I have the power to love, to forgive, to be kind in this situation." Through this recognition of God, we practice His presence, and His light shines in the darkness.

Day 31

Filled Full

See to it that no one takes you captive by philosophy and
empty deceit, according to human tradition, according
to the elemental spirits of the world, and not according
to Christ. For in him the whole fullness of deity dwells
bodily, and you have been filled in him, who is the head
of all rule and authority.

COLOSSIANS 2:8-10 ESV

The Greek words for "fullness," *pleroma*,[1] and "filled," *pleroo*,[2] are used in various places. A ship is "filled" on the dock with everything it needs for the long voyage. Twelve baskets were filled full of extra loaves and fish after the miracle (Matt. 14:20). Love one another, for love is the filling up of the law (Rom. 13:10). These words speak of abundance. Jesus said, "I have come so that they may have life, and may have it abundantly" (John 10:10 NET). And the word Jesus used for "abundant" means over and above, more than is necessary, superior, and extraordinary.[3]

I have come that they may have superior life, a life over and above what is necessary, extraordinary life, filled full, overflowing.

If all the fullness of the Godhead lives in Christ in bodily form, and I am filled full in Christ, the fullness of the Godhead lives in me as everything I need for the long voyage. I'm fully packed with what I need.

The gospel is a whole new realm where we have access to the power to love even our enemies because we contain the One who is love (1 John 4:12). We have the power to forgive because we contain the Forgiver. We have the power to bring reconciliation because we contain the Reconciler (2 Cor. 5:19).

The gospel—the good news—connects God's life and resources with our limitations, where our childlike dependence meets the Father's superabundant life and the rivers of living water. Jesus was asked, "'What shall we do, that we may work the works of God?' Jesus answered and said to them, 'This is the work of God, that you believe in Him whom He sent'" (John 6:28–29).

> *The gospel—the good news—connects God's life and resources with our limitations, where our childlike dependence meets the Father's superabundant life and the rivers of living water.*

There's only one thing *we* do, at the source, in the depths. We rely on and wholly trust ourselves to the One God has sent to live in our hearts. "So then faith comes by hearing, and hearing by the word of God" (Rom. 10:17).

Ignoring "Christ in you, the hope of glory"—the actual, living, vibrant life of God in us—keeps us as powerless believers stuck on an endless hamster wheel of our own effort, trying to achieve what is impossible by human power. "The thief comes only to steal and kill and destroy; I have come so that they may have life, and may have it abundantly" (John 10:10 NET).

If there is a central truth that all hell seeks to hide and subvert, it's the abundant life we already possess right this moment in Christ, the life that flows from the unstoppable, eternal love of God for us. Believing I am independent and "trying to be like Christ" stops the flow of love, joy, peace, patience, gentleness, goodness, humility, faith, and self-control that are already ours in Him.

We can know we are abiding if we are loving God and others with love, joy, peace, patience, gentleness, goodness, humility, faith, and self-control. We're often tempted to try to *do* all those things to prove we're abiding. This stops our abiding because we're right back into trusting ourselves.

To live without depending on God makes us subject to the winds of society, the approval of friends, every wound from our enemies, and every word of the tempter.

Peter wrote, "His divine power has bestowed on us everything necessary for life and godliness through the rich knowledge of the one who called us by his own glory and excellence" (2 Peter 1:3 NET). We have everything we need, right this moment, for life and godliness.

Christ in us is our total fullness and sufficiency in every situation because we were packed full for the voyage at the docks.

Day 32

Dearly Loved

Therefore, be imitators of God as dearly loved children.

EPHESIANS 5:1 NET

You are God's dearly loved child. You're not just *tolerated* by Him. He loves you as you would love your own child, only infinitely more. We can live every day as God's dear children.

Have you ever been awakened in the middle of the night with a bunch of words in your head telling you that you're nobody, that you'll never amount to anything, that you're an imposter, that no one loves you, that you're stupid, or bad, or that your sins keep you from God? All of these are lies because you are God's precious, beloved child.

How would you feel if your child or a child you dearly loved was believing these things? What would you do?

We're destined to be dearly loved forever, from now through

every moment, to be disciplined, guided, and corrected, destined to *overcome.*

Remember the past. The first generation of Hebrews out of Egypt believed the flood of lies coming into their heads: *They're giants. We're nothing. We're little bugs to be squashed. We're just slaves, not warriors. Life was better in Egypt; at least we were safe and had good food. These warriors in the promised land are going to slaughter us.*

Say these truths, not just with your mind but with your mouth, to God:

Thank You for loving me and giving Your Son for me (John 3:16).

Thank You for choosing me as Your dear child (1 John 3:1).

Thank You for buying me with a price. I'm not my own; I belong to You (1 Cor. 6:19–20).

Thank You for justifying me and redeeming me (Rom. 3:24).

Thank You that by one offering, You have perfected me forever, that in every moment You are sanctifying me (Heb. 10:14).

Thank You that I have everything I need right now for *life* and *godliness* in Christ (2 Peter 1:3).

You have not given me a spirit of fear; thank You for Your Spirit of power and of love and of a sound mind (2 Tim. 1:7).

Thank You for giving me full access to come boldly before Your throne to receive Your mercy and Your *charis*—grace, favor, and power—to help in time of need (Heb. 4:16).

Thank You, Father, that in Christ all the fullness of the Godhead lives in bodily form, and I am filled full in Him (Col. 2:9).

These are not things we *strive to become.* This reality of Christ in us is the root of *who we are;* this is our starting place, the ground and source of our being. All Christians stand on equal footing. We all have the same Spirit.

You might think, *Yes, but you don't understand how hard it is for me because* _____. Or, *Yes, but my theology says* _____.

Yes, I know. I've had all my buts, too. No matter what our upbringing, our experiences, our traumas, we all have our own giants to slay in our promised land. None of us are let off the hook here. And if we have the courage to believe it, the Son of God Himself lives inside us as the author and finisher of faith. He's our faith-generator (Gal. 2:20; 5:22).

Those lies, those thoughts out of nowhere that nip and slash, dogs biting at our heels, trying to drag us down into the mud—all we do is reach our arms up to our Father and look Him full in the face. The dogs run. The lies begin to dissipate.

In C. S. Lewis's Chronicles of Narnia, in *The Silver Chair*, Puddleglum the Marsh-wiggle stamps out the witch's fire. Rousing himself from her enchantment, he says,

> "Suppose this black pit of a kingdom of yours *is* the only world. Well, it strikes me as a pretty poor one. And that's a funny thing, when you come to think of it. We're just babies making up a game, if you're right. But four babies playing a game can make a play-world which licks your real world hollow. That's why I'm going to stand by the play-world. I'm on Aslan's side even if there isn't any Aslan to lead it. I'm going to live as like a Narnian as I can even if there isn't any Narnia."[1]

We rouse ourselves and wake from the lies. We can respond with the encouragement from the book of Hebrews: "Therefore we also, since we are surrounded by so great a cloud of witnesses, let

Those lies, those thoughts out of nowhere that nip and slash, dogs biting at our heels, trying to drag us down into the mud— all we do is reach our arms up to our Father and look Him full in the face.

us lay aside every weight, and the sin which so easily ensnares us, and let us run with endurance the race that is set before us" (Heb. 12:1). We run into God's arms and into His heart.

Lay aside every weight. Stamp out the enchanting fire. "Casting down arguments and every high thing that exalts itself against the knowledge of God, bringing every thought into captivity to the obedience of Christ" (2 Cor. 10:5).

"Awake, you who sleep,
Arise from the dead
And Christ will give you light." (Eph. 5:14)

Day 33

A New Heart

> "I will give you a new heart and put a new spirit within
> you; I will take the heart of stone out of your flesh and
> give you a heart of flesh. I will put My Spirit within you
> and cause you to walk in My statutes, and you will keep
> My judgments and do them."
>
> EZEKIEL 36:26-27

Believers often quote, "The heart is deceitful . . . and desperately wicked" (Jer. 17:9), but Ezekiel prophesied a time when a new heart and a new spirit would be given to us—the Lord's very own Holy Spirit. This time began two thousand years ago. "Therefore, if anyone is in Christ, he is a new creation; old things have passed away; behold, all things have become new" (2 Cor. 5:17).

Many of us continue to live for years under sin-consciousness, hating ourselves, frustrated, not doing the good we should, doing what we hate, and hating what we do. We're focused on what we call "my self," unaware that the thoughts, attitudes, and actions of the self we're hating come from living in the shadow of the law—a frustrated, "independent me" trying to be good—rather than abiding, resting, and living from the goodness of God in us.

> For since the law has but a shadow of the good things to come instead of the true form of these realities, it can never, by the same sacrifices that are continually offered every year, make perfect those who draw near. Otherwise, would they not have ceased to be offered, since the worshipers, having once been cleansed, would no longer have any consciousness of sins? (Heb. 10:1–2 ESV)

Life under the law had no real resolution and no power, only a shadow. Jesus brought the reality. "But when Christ had offered for all time a single sacrifice for sins, he sat down at the right hand of God, waiting from that time until his enemies should be made a footstool for his feet. For by a single offering he has perfected for all time those who are being sanctified" (Heb. 10:12–14 ESV).

By that offering made once for all time, we are cleansed once for all time and need only to wash our feet after the day's walk.

By that offering made once for all time, we are cleansed once for all time and need only to wash our feet after the day's walk (John 13:10). We are no longer to live in sin-consciousness, constantly fearing and self-condemning. Jesus made a single sacrifice, crying, "It is finished!" Not only are our *sins* taken care of—the actions—but Jesus killed the root of sins, the old union (Eph. 2:2) that produced sins. The Holy Spirit now lives in us to continually sanctify—that is, He makes us holy, set apart, manifesting in us the Spirit's love, joy, peace, patience, goodness, kindness, gentleness, humility, faith, and self-control. By this Holy Spirit God Himself will *cause* us to walk in His statutes, His tasks, His decrees. "I will put My Spirit within you and cause you to walk in My statutes, and you will keep My judgments and do them" (Ezek. 36:27). For God to *cause* us to walk in His ways is very different than trying hard *by our effort* to read the Bible, write lists, and do what God says. Ezekiel says we will keep His judgments—that is, we'll hang on to His ways of thinking, His decisions, and we'll walk in those directions—through the Spirit.

The apostle Paul warned of attitudes of approaching God by rules and regulations: "Beware lest anyone cheat you through philosophy and empty deceit, according to the tradition of men, according to the basic principles of the world, and not according to Christ. For in Him dwells all the fullness of the Godhead bodily; and you are complete in Him, who is the head of all principality and power" (Col. 2:8–10). What is the centerpiece of the tradition of men, and the most basic principle of the world? *Work by the sweat of your brow* (Gen. 3:19). In a word, independence. *It's all up to you.*

Don't let this lie cheat you. Paul tells us we are right now filled and fueled by the God who is Love—the love inside us—and love is the fulfilling of the law. We've had a heart change.

But this isn't automatic. We're not robots, and passivity has no place in the kingdom. As His sons and daughters in Christ He has given us relationship and fellowship with Himself as a gift, a privilege, and a right. He is our Father, no matter what comes, and we can have fellowship with Him at any moment. We are to "come boldly to the throne of grace, that we may obtain mercy and find grace to help in time of need" (Heb. 4:16).

This fellowship begins to fuel our thoughts, our attitudes, our doings. We begin to see how beautiful God is, how loving, how kind, how faithful, and we soon want to become like Him. Through this process God captivates our *want*; He gives vision of what our future can be, and our *will* soon follows. This is how He *causes* us to walk in His ways of thinking, being, and doing without forcing us.

Jesus is the door into this life of walking with God. He's the source of our new hearts, and we're the expressions of that source. If we live in Him, dwell with Him, and He lives in and dwells with us, we will bear much fruit (John 15:5). *This is the fruit of the fellowship of abiding dependence.*

Day 34

Children of Light

For you are all children of light, children of the day. We
are not of the night or of the darkness. So then let us not
sleep, as others do, but let us keep awake and be sober.

1 THESSALONIANS 5:5-6 ESV

We have been reborn as children of light into "a new and living way," and we're to stay awake in that—calm, collected, eyes open, and clearheaded. Stay awake to grace, favor, and power.

Through His life, death, resurrection, and ascension, Jesus opened a new way—a new and living way and not the old, dead way. Our new way is alive with life and light, not based on fleshly goodness but rooted in our relationship with God; it flows from daily, vibrant fellowship with Him.

The old way of the law was based on human beings trying diligently by their own power to obey. Moses said, "Now it shall come to pass, if you diligently obey the voice of the LORD your God, to observe carefully all His commandments which I command you

163

today, that the LORD your God will set you high above all nations of the earth" (Deut. 28:1). Blessings followed this diligence of doing *if* the doer carefully observed *all* God's commandments—not some, but all. That's a lot of pressure.

Moses continued: "But it shall come to pass, if you do not obey the voice of the LORD your God, to observe carefully all His commandments and His statutes which I command you today, that all these curses will come upon you and overtake you" (Deut. 28:15). And the list of curses is comprehensive. There are *fifty-two hair-raising verses* after Deuteronomy 28:15 delineating the dire consequences for not keeping *all* the commandments. So God, through Moses, gave a complex system of sacrifices to pay for transgressing the law and sinning against God and others.

The old and dead way imposed external commands upon straining human selves, producing fear of failure, sin, self-condemnation, and sin-consciousness—darkness. It grew pride and self-congratulation—darkness. Under the law, self-effort was the starting place, and there was no way out of sin-consciousness; the sacrifices *reminded* the people of their sins.

In the new and living way, Jesus made one sacrifice for all time for everyone. In Him, we're born again as sons and daughters of light, filled with the Holy Spirit. We're given a new union and a new identity; our starting place is the fullness and sufficiency of Christ in us. The living law, the living Word, is written on our new hearts.

John says in his epistle, "This is the message which we have heard from Him and declare to you, that God is light and in Him is no darkness at all. If we say that we have fellowship with Him, and walk in darkness, we lie and do not practice the truth. But if we walk in the light as He is in the light, we have fellowship with one another, and the blood of Jesus Christ His Son cleanses us from all sin" (1 John 1:5–7).

If we're walking in the dark, it's much easier to trip and fall. We can't tell friend from foe, and we're vulnerable to attack. In the darkness, we often break things unintentionally by running into them, and it's tough to locate food or water.

Back when I believed I had to please God by trying hard, I avoided, skimmed over, and even disliked verses like John's. I couldn't see clearly because I wasn't walking in the light; I didn't know He lived in me. But John's words aren't a prompt to try harder; they're a diagnostic tool for us to see whether we're really walking with God. It's an impossibility for anyone to be walking in darkness and having fellowship with Christ at the same time. The verb tense says if we say we are having fellowship with Him *right now*, and we're walking in darkness, we're not telling the truth.

As I began walking more consistently with God (though I still forget), I was glad I had a diagnostic tool to know when I had stepped out of abiding. Whatever is opposite of love, joy, peace, patience, gentleness, goodness, humility, faith, and self-control is darkness. When I am walking in darkness, it's a signal to let me know I've stepped out of the light.

Now, I don't mean unpleasant or negative feelings are *bad*. Feelings just *are*, like the weather. We're going to have negative feelings, and we can admit it when we have them. The diagnostic is helpful, though, to show when we've begun to hold on to them, chew on them, and ruminate—when we *feed* on our bad feelings—until the darkness begins to spin and spread out into our attitudes and actions. Sometimes we need wise counsel from others to help us see again.

When we step out of abiding, God has no condemnation for us (Rom. 8:1). We simply step back into the light with Him. He forgives us when we sin, just as the father's forgiveness was waiting for the prodigal son after he went astray (Luke 15:11–32). But the son only had to return to receive it; he had to come face-to-face with his father again to see and receive forgiveness. Immediately, the father offered the ring, robe, sandals, and a big party. The father didn't punish him or put him in second class but embraced him as a son and returned to him the privileges that accompany it.

We already have complete and full forgiveness in Christ, but confession is good for *us*. It opens the way for us to *receive* God's forgiveness, and it clears the way for new life. To be a child of light means we *can* walk in the light with God. We're the child; He's the light. This means we're no longer walking blind; we can see rather than tripping and falling over every obstacle of temptation or tumbling into every hole in the ground. It means we see and know that our Father is love, that He loves us and others, and that He's in us and will be our love for others, our joy, peace, and all the rest.

> We already have complete and full forgiveness in Christ, but confession is good for us. It opens the way for us to receive God's forgiveness, and it clears the way for new life.

Prevention is the best cure. Stay awake to God in you. We are children of light; we're to believe it and trust the One in us who is light and life, living from Him. Walking in the light will drive our thoughts, attitudes, and actions. Our part is to keep our eyes open to Christ in us and who we are in Him; after all, "The eye is the lamp of the body. So, if your eye is healthy, your whole body will be full of light" (Matt. 6:22 ESV).

Day 35

Fire

And the Angel of the LORD appeared to him in a flame
of fire from the midst of a bush. So he looked,
and behold, the bush was burning with fire,
but the bush was not consumed.

EXODUS 3:2

Moses stared at the bush that wouldn't burn up, and God's voice lit his heart to lead the Hebrews out of Egypt (Ex. 3:2). The book of Acts records that fire appeared when the Holy Spirit descended on the disciples on the day of Pentecost (Acts 2:3). This fire of God filled Peter with courage as he stood and preached to the people of Judea and Jerusalem. The Holy Spirit lit up the hearts of the crowd, and three thousand people came into relationship and fellowship with Jesus (Acts 2:14–21, 41).

Author and founder of OMS International, Mrs. Charles E. Cowman, wrote, "We are kindled that we might kindle others."[1]

Contact with God, daily life with Him, transforms us. When

we are actively *knowing* Him, He burns up false, petty, small ways of living—hatreds, jealousies, envy, gossip, and slander. "For our God is a consuming fire" (Heb. 12:29). He burns up our little fears and gives us courage to stare down our big ones. If I'm facing off with a mighty Goliath, alone, with a sling and a stone, I'll run away out of fear. But if I face the very same Goliath as I'm walking with a real, present, and almighty God, and I am *knowing* Him through the whole experience, I'm much less susceptible to fear. In knowing God, the reality of His presence, love, strength, and power are greater to me than the situation—and a sling and a stone will suffice.

> *In knowing God, the reality of His presence, love, strength, and power are greater to me than the situation—and a sling and a stone will suffice.*

This stoking of our hearts isn't intellectual, though it uses the intellect. It isn't caused solely by studying the Bible, though it often uses the Bible to stir the flame and focus the heat. This fire leaping up isn't just a feeling or emotion, though it very often brings emotions.

To get an ideal, fully realized picture of what this fire looks like in a human, the apostle John describes the ascended Jesus: "His head and hair were white like wool, as white as snow, and His eyes like a flame of fire. . . . His countenance was like the sun shining in its strength" (Rev. 1:14, 16).

Here is the Son of God, filled with the fire that doesn't burn Him up. John continues, "And when I saw Him, I fell at His feet as dead. But He laid His right hand on me, saying to me, 'Do not be afraid; I am the First and the Last. I am He who lives, and was dead, and behold, I am alive forevermore. Amen. And I have the keys of Hades and of Death'" (Rev. 1:17–18).

This is the Christ we are *in*, and He is in us—this Person with all love, light, kindness, love, eternal life, and power, filled with the fire of God.

The apostle Paul prayed for us,

> For this reason I bow my knees to the Father of our Lord Jesus Christ, from whom the whole family in heaven and earth is named, that He would grant you, according to the riches of His glory, to be strengthened with might through His Spirit in the inner man, that Christ may dwell in your hearts through faith; that you, being rooted and grounded in love, may be able to comprehend with all the saints what is the width and length and depth and height—to know the love of Christ which passes knowledge; that you may be filled with all the fullness of God.
>
> Now to Him who is able to do exceedingly abundantly above all that we ask or think, according to the power that works in us, to Him be glory in the church by Christ Jesus to all generations, forever and ever. Amen. (Eph. 3:14–21)

What would our lives look like if we lived knowing we're filled with this fire of God's Spirit daily? Paul says Christ dwells in our hearts through faith. It is this faith-recognition of His indwelling presence that causes the fire of His presence to grow and expand in us.

What if we began to recognize Him inside us as the source and ground of our very being, our rock in every situation? What if we turned to Him every time we had bad thoughts, anxieties, fears, doubts, temptations, and asked Him to burn them up in the fire of His love, of His joy, of His power?

What will we see in our lives if we live like Mary did and sit at His feet? What if we take God at His word, if we recognize these deepest truths, if we trust the warming fire of the Holy Spirit as the root and ground of our being?

We'll be able to love others, even when they are against us. It won't be based on *trying* to love; it'll be rooted in knowing Christ in us as our life, and that God loves the other person. We'll more often experience an increasing sense of peace, even in trying circumstances. We'll have a sense of joy; even when things go badly, we can know God is redeeming situations, growing us up as His sons and daughters, bringing new possibilities into our paths.

God doesn't see us just as we are in this moment. As the ideal Father, He's also thinking of what we will be. And He's not only thinking of what we will be, but of how we are now growing[2]— growing in experiencing the love of Christ which is beyond intellectual knowledge, growing "till we all come to the unity of the faith and of the knowledge of the Son of God, to a perfect man, to the measure of the stature of the fullness of Christ" (Eph. 4:13). God's love-purpose is that we would increasingly be filled with and live from everything He is in us.

George MacDonald wrote, "For love loves unto purity. Love has ever in view the absolute loveliness of that which it beholds. . . . Therefore all that is not beautiful in the beloved, all that comes between and is not of love's kind, must be destroyed . . . [for] our God is a consuming fire."[3]

Day 36

Courage to Leap

Your ears shall hear a word behind you, saying,
"This is the way, walk in it,"
Whenever you turn to the right hand
Or whenever you turn to the left.

ISAIAH 30:21

No apologetics, reason, or logic can take us all the way into living in the Spirit. They can bring us as close as we can get to certainty. But then there's always a leap.

We can read, study, pray, strive, try hard, fail, try hard again, fail, and try again. We can learn all about our psychology, take personality tests, and dig into our past. These can all be good things—until they begin to usurp the place of the leap. These things can take us only so far; they bring us to the edge of a precipice. In the life of the Spirit, there is no such thing as absolute intellectual certainty. Sarah laughed at the promise of a son; Moses didn't at first believe he was the right choice for delivering the Hebrews from

Egypt, making excuse after excuse; when we read David's psalms, we recognize that "the man after God's own heart" had to *choose* childlike trust in God rather than trusting his own perceptions of his life—just as we do.

When circumstances, reason, and logic get us to the edge, we always have a choice to leap and fly or to shrink back. We stand on the edge and feel the rush of the updrafts, see the distant mountains, the fields of grass far below, and it can be dizzying. It's simultaneously thrilling and terrifying, yet we have to choose: we listen, relying on the God who has taken us to this vantage point and go forward, or we go back, relying on our own seeing, our own ways, our own means. We'll often have opposition from those around us.

In C. S. Lewis's second Narnia book, *Prince Caspian,* the four Pevensie children are with Trumpkin the Dwarf, trying to find a way through rugged country to meet up with Caspian and the others. They come upon a gorge, and Peter begins to lead them down.

Lucy, the youngest, sees Aslan the great Lion a little way off going *up,* wanting them to follow. She alerts the others, but they can't see him, so they don't believe her. The matter comes to a vote; everyone is tired, wanting to go down rather than up, and Lucy loses. They go way down the gorge; the beauty is delightful for a while, and they're cheered to see the town of Beruna in the distance. But soon they're attacked by a barrage of enemy arrows, forcing their retreat all the way up the gorge.

Back at the top, they set up camp. Lucy wakes up in the night, gets up and goes wandering, and has an encounter with Aslan. After her joy at seeing him, and sweet communion together, he begins to tell her what she must do.

"Lucy," he said, "You have work in hand, and much time has been lost today. . . . If you go back to the others now, and wake them up; and tell them you have seen me again; and that you must all get up at once and follow me—what will happen? There is only one way of finding out."

"Do you mean that is what you want me to do?" gasped Lucy.

"Yes, little one," said Aslan.

"Will the others see you too?" asked Lucy.

"Certainly not at first," said Aslan. "Later on, it depends."

"But they won't believe me!" said Lucy.

"It doesn't matter," said Aslan.

"Oh dear, oh dear," said Lucy. . . . Lucy buried her head in his mane to hide from his face. But there must have been magic in his mane. She could feel lion-strength going into her. Quite suddenly she sat up.

"I'm sorry, Aslan," she said. "I'm ready now."

"Now you are a lioness," said Aslan. "And now all Narnia will be renewed. But come. We have no time to lose."[1]

In Aslan, Lucy finds the courage to go against even those she loves, following Aslan, and leading them all to safety.

In those moments on the cliff edge, times of opposition from others, of decisions whether to leap or go up or down, right or left, the most crucial thing is to take a moment to commune with Jesus, to look into the face of God, to be enveloped by His presence, to come boldly before the throne of grace to be filled with faith, courage, and instruction.

Day 37

Perceptions

God is our refuge and strength,
a very present help in trouble.
Therefore we will not fear though
the earth gives way,
though the mountains be moved
into the heart of the sea.

PSALMS 46:1-2 ESV

If a neighbor called tonight and said, "There's a man with a gun hiding on your porch," we'd have an emotional response. Fear? Trembling anxiety? Anger? Potential scenarios would flood our brain, tending to overwhelm calm thinking. These feelings would be real to us, and unless we were trained military personnel, it would be hard to keep them from clouding our judgment.

Imagine the neighbor calling ten minutes later to tell you he was wrong. It was just a shadow from your magnolia tree blowing in the wind. The feelings would have been real, as in existing inside you, producing adrenaline, those butterflies in your gut, the shaking in your hands. You'd have made plans based on false information—the false alarms of a failed system.

Jesus said, "The lamp of the body is the eye. If therefore your eye is good, your whole body will be full of light. But if your eye is bad, your whole body will be full of darkness" (Matt. 6:22–23). The way we perceive reality matters.

If our perceptions about reality are wrong, our feelings lie, and we live, act, and make plans from fear. Jesus came to give sight to the blind, to those who can't see reality as God sees—to those walking in darkness. "Where there is no vision, the people perish" (Prov. 29:18 KJV).

These days we have twenty-four-hour news services feeding us a constant torrent of negatives. Eating this information daily produces thoughts and overall perceptions of the world in our minds, bringing in fear of the future, anger, hatred, and wretched anxiety. We live from these feelings, self-medicate, make life choices, and treat others based on how we feel. It's confusing, mind-numbing, and awful.

God invites us into a daily walk with Him to see life and circumstances His way, a walk marked by real life and peace.

The Bible calls this "walking after the flesh," when we live life as though we're our own starting point, having to navigate life by our own self-power and effort. "For to set the mind on the flesh is death, but to set the mind on the Spirit is life and peace" (Rom. 8:6 ESV).

God invites us into a daily walk with Him to see life and circumstances His way, a walk marked by real life and peace—life that is truly alive because it is

God Himself, peace that is God's own eternal peace, not the circumstantial, tenuous peace of the world. This daily walk of fellowship involves adjusting our perceptions and our mindset to see from His perspective.

The author of Psalm 46 tells us God is our shelter and bold strength, abundantly present, ready to give aid when we're in dire straits. For this reason, we will not allow ourselves to be full of dread or fear, or be overawed, even though the ground gives way beneath us and the mountains crumble into the sea. Let it drop. Abandon it. Let it alone. Relax. Be quiet and know that He is God. He will be uplifted among the nations. He will be uplifted in the whole earth. See reality as God sees it.

The almost fantastical thing is this God is *in you*, in Christ, by the Holy Spirit. He is the light of the world. Whether we live from this God-life involves changing our perceptions. It involves our mindset. And that involves abiding dependence.

Day 38

Mindset and Renewal

I beseech you therefore, brethren, by the mercies of God,
that you present your bodies a living sacrifice, holy,
acceptable to God, which is your reasonable service. And
do not be conformed to this world, but be *transformed by
the renewing of your mind*, that you may prove what is
that good and acceptable and perfect will of God.

ROMANS 12:1-2

For to set the mind on the flesh is death, but to *set the
mind on the Spirit is life* and peace.

ROMANS 8:6 ESV

Rest always comes before doing. We go to bed early because
tomorrow will be a long day of work. We "tank up" on food, too;
we eat before starting a day of hard physical work.

In sports, in music, in life, our thoughts can sustain us or poison us. What we believe about ourselves will affect the outcome
of the race, the show, the business meeting, and eventually the

career. The thoughts we carry around affect our relationships, our children, our friends—they affect the world.

The apostle Paul says we are to renew our minds, that this mind-renewal causes transformation in our attitudes and actions. Our minds and hearts require food, and this is their best food—Jesus. Eating renews our strength so that we can mount up with wings as eagles.

It's easy for us—raised in a world of doing, running to and fro, and busyness—to skim crucial, life-giving passages of Scripture to get to the "do" verses. Verbs like *do* or *do not* are eye candy for the doers among us. We rush off without eating; we start the day without mind renewal. Ready, aim, fire. It seems easier, but whenever we begin to *do* without first setting our minds on who God is and who we are in Him, we're setting ourselves up for frustration.

If we can live God's kind of life—love, joy, peace—by our own power, then Jesus died for nothing (Gal. 2:21).

In the new covenant, doing comes *after* recognizing who God is, what He has done, and who He is in us. We ask, "Who is God? Where is God? What has God done on my behalf? Who am I in Him?" This is mind renewal. It is mind-setting. We feast on God's view of everything and set our hearts on things above.

In Colossians, Paul says we are to be "giving thanks to the Father who has qualified us to be partakers of the inheritance of the saints in the light. He has delivered us from the power of darkness and conveyed us into the kingdom of the Son of His love, in whom we have redemption through His blood, the forgiveness of sins" (Col. 1:12–14).

Paul continues. Christ in us is the hope of glory, of luminescence, that in Christ dwells all the fullness of the Godhead bodily;

and we are complete (filled full) in Him (Col. 2:10).

In Christ, we were spiritually circumcised by God as we were buried with Him. The old self, the old union, was cut off and thrown out. We were raised with Christ. We were made alive together with Him, and He forgave all our trespasses (Col. 2:11–13).

All legal requirements for relationship with God were nailed to the cross and taken out of the way, forever (Col. 2:14). Therefore, we're not to allow anyone to set legal requirements for relationship and fellowship with God. Rules, regulations, and observances were shadows of things which were to come. Now the substance is here: Christ, and Christ in you. Let no one cheat you of this (Col. 2:16–23).

"I am the bread of life. He who comes to Me shall never hunger, and he who believes in Me shall never thirst" (John 6:35).

We entrust ourselves to our meals every day. We get hungry, see what food is available, and then we take, and eat. The food then takes us—it nourishes and upholds

Jesus is our food and drink; we come to Him daily, frequently, boldly, for everything we need.

our strength, and our body builds its new cells on the quality of the food it is given. Jesus is our food and drink; we come to Him daily, frequently, boldly, for everything we need—we take, and eat, and He takes us. He sustains us, and His life becomes the very bone of our bone, flesh of our flesh. This is our renewal, every day.

Jesus said it clearly: "He who eats My flesh and drinks My blood abides in Me, and I in him" (John 6:56). The foundation of abiding in Christ is to come to Him, take, and eat and drink. This is not merely a ceremony, a ritual, or even what we call the Lord's

Supper or Communion; the ceremony renews our minds and hearts to true reality—the whole point. Jesus passed the bread and wine around to the disciples and said, "Do this in remembrance of Me." By recognizing Him as real and present, as our Source, we are feeding on heavenly bread and wine.

Day 39

Receiving
and Reigning

> For if by the one man's offense death reigned through the
> one, much more those who receive abundance of grace
> and of the gift of righteousness will reign in life through
> the One, Jesus Christ.
>
> ROMANS 5:17

What would it look like to reign in life through the One, Jesus Christ?

"But the fruit of the Spirit is love, joy, peace, patience, kindness, goodness, faithfulness, gentleness, self-control; against such things there is no law" (Gal. 5:22–23 ESV). Reigning looks like the increase of these qualities in our lives so that others can experience them. Peaches on a tree are visible. They hang off the branches, available for others to eat or reject. They give nourishment and the taste is sublime.

If we're reigning in life, and people around us are getting out of control, we can control ourselves through trusting the indwelling life of the One, Jesus Christ. If we're tempted to be unkind or harsh, we can be gentle—through relying on the One living in us. In a bad situation, we'd have a deep, settled sense of peace, regardless of our emotions; we are "casting all [our] care upon Him" (1 Peter 5:7) because we know He takes care of us.

Reigning in life looks like the fruit of the Spirit, the opposite of the fruit of self-effort. We often *try* to reign in life. We read about the fruit of the Spirit and think, "I'll try to be more loving, more joyful, more patient." We try harder, pray more, do more, and eventually we burn out. It's empty. It doesn't work; the branches of a peach tree don't pull themselves off the tree and *try* to produce fruit. They rest in the tree and receive. Rain falls, the sun shines, the roots and trunk do their work, and new buds appear.

"Those who receive abundance of grace and of the gift of righteousness will reign in life through the One, Jesus Christ" (Rom. 5:17).

The word "receive" is a verb; the present tense and active voice of the Greek in the verse above mean something more like, "Those who are actively receiving abundance of grace and of the gift of righteousness will reign in life."

Receiving isn't transactional. The prodigal son wanted a single transaction with his father: "Give me what I am owed." Then he left, no longer wanting the relationship. The father gave and the son received, but he couldn't carry away unlimited resources with one transaction.

When he ran out of money and came back, the father gave him the source of unlimited resources—the father gave himself. The father was the head of an estate with hired workers. For the son to have access to these unlimited resources, he had to be living *with* his father on the estate. He had to continually be receiving. The father was always ready to give, but the son had to humble himself and recognize his father as the source of all.

We actively and continually receive the resources of our Father when we live with Him, in Him, having Himself in us in Christ. Our "work" is to recognize Him as our source of all and to walk with Him.

This recognition, this fellowship, is something we *practice*, and as we practice, we get better at it. It's really the one thing we *do* with God. We connect in our need to His supply, in weakness to His strength. He gives, and we receive.

The resources of God come in handy. If we're carrying unforgiveness, we can turn inwardly to God and tell Him so. I've often prayed, "I forgive them with your Spirit's forgiveness in me, but you're going to have to change how I feel." Then I leave the feelings up to Him and walk in trust that when I see that person the love and grace of God for them will be active in me.

We'll forget at times, slip back into self-effort, and make mistakes, but it will all go toward teaching us that the recognition of the life and resources we've received comes before reigning. We recognize God has given us Himself, and then we reign by walking in Him.

Day 40

Peter, the Rock

Simon Peter answered and said,
"You are the Christ, the Son of the living God."
Jesus answered and said to him, "Blessed are you, Simon
Bar-Jonah, for flesh and blood has not revealed this
to you, but My Father who is in heaven. And I also say to
you that you are Peter, and on this rock I will
build My church, and the gates of Hades
shall not prevail against it."

MATTHEW 16:16-18

P eter's name, *petros*, means "rock" or "stone."[1] At that time, and until the resurrection, Peter was anything but a rock. He wasn't solid and dependable, but fickle and unreliable. He blurted out foolish, awkward things, trusted Jesus only to a point, and boasted about his own to-the-death loyalty. Peter in the Gospels lived by his fleshly abilities, his own seeing, his own ways of coping.

But Jesus saw Peter moving toward a destiny, a future built on the God-given awareness that Jesus is the Messiah, the Christ, the

Son of the living God. Jesus saw Peter not just as he was, but as he would be, that all of Peter's foolishness and self-belief, culminating in his betrayals, was going to be used for good; Peter would be crushed by his own wretched behavior, the bitter fruit of attitudes likely held since childhood.

When Jesus rose from the dead, the angel at the tomb told Mary Magdalene and the other two women, "Go, tell His disciples—and Peter—that He is going before you into Galilee; there you will see Him, as He said to you" (Mark 16:7).

The brash, get-it-done Peter of the Gospels, the rock who crumbled under pressure, is transformed into one of the unbroken granite pillars of the early church.

Jesus reached out in love, grace, and mercy to Peter the rock, still calling him by his true name. After Pentecost, in the book of Acts, we see a totally different Peter, filled with the Holy Spirit, confidently preaching to the crowds, healing, and teaching. The brash, get-it-done Peter of the Gospels, the rock who crumbled under pressure, is transformed into one of the unbroken granite pillars of the early church.

You and I are on a journey with God, my friend. Most of us start like Peter, full of vim and vigor, with all our baggage from trying to get through life. As we age, we all look back and regret things we've said and done—or didn't say and do.

But God *sees reality as it is*. He's not interested in patching up the old self, with all its distorted ideas of reality. The old version of Peter was crushed to death by his own behavior, because an independent self is really depending on everything in the world but God. That Peter died on the cross with Jesus.

At the resurrection of Jesus, God created a new version of

Peter—not merely improved, but a new creation, and at Pentecost we see Peter infused with God's Holy Spirit. In preaching to the crowds His boldness is real, and his confidence makes him concise and to the point.

But even then, Peter had to *learn* how to walk in the Spirit, just as we do, and Galatians 2 shows he still had his bad moments dealing with fear, especially fear of what others thought of him. Paul writes,

> But when Peter came to Antioch, I had to oppose him to his face, for what he did was very wrong. When he first arrived, he ate with the Gentile believers, who were not circumcised. But afterward, when some friends of James came, Peter wouldn't eat with the Gentiles anymore. He was afraid of criticism from these people who insisted on the necessity of circumcision. As a result, other Jewish believers followed Peter's hypocrisy, and even Barnabas was led astray by their hypocrisy. (Gal. 2:11–13 NLT)

Peter's old habit of self-reliance reasserted itself in a stressful situation, and Paul called him out on it.

But God redeemed Peter's failures and has used them for centuries to encourage us to know our failures don't sever our relationship with God, that we can reenter fellowship with God simply by turning to Him—*metanoia*—and accepting His forgiveness. Then we make amends to anyone we've hurt, get wise counsel if necessary, and move forward in reliant trust and dependence.

As with Peter, God created new versions of us at the cross too, and if we know Jesus we've already experienced them to varying degrees. We've felt the sweet breath of joy even in tough times; we've had a settled inner *knowing* that God is with us in a bad situation, that He would bring us through it. We've known His mercy, kindness, and forgiveness. We've felt His love come through us to others, and we've seen resurrections in our lives again and again, where things we thought were dead and gone are filled with new life and come back to us.

And we've failed, too, like Peter, acting from fear, unbelief, flesh-effort, and all the rest. *Yet God redeems all of it.* What counts is growth, and growth comes from a branch being connected. "What is important is faith expressing itself in love" (Gal. 5:6 NLT). Reliance on God produces inner fruit and outer action. It brings love for God and love for people.

There's more for us up ahead; these breaths of joy, the moments when we're caught up in worship, when we love others well—these moments are meant to grow and expand. We have been blessed with all spiritual blessings, we're sons, daughters, heirs of God and co-heirs with Christ. Christ lives in us. We have been given everything, and you can't get more than everything.

But we *can* appropriate and experience more of who He is in us and through us. If I've been given ten million dollars, I don't need more; I need training in how to manage, utilize, and grow what I have been given.

Jesus said He came that we might have life and have it to the full, that rivers of living water would flow from our inmost being. As we learn to walk and mature in the Holy Spirit, He guides us and teaches us how to use the resources of God for His good purposes. Like Peter, the rock, we're destined to overcome as we learn to walk and mature in abiding dependence.

Afterword

Life with or without God is an adventure. Adventures have plenty of long, dull days of travel across uninteresting landscapes. They can lead through mosquito-ridden wetlands, tough mountain ranges, or arid deserts with poisonous snakes. A good adventure has its share of fistfights, skirmishes, and full-on battles. There are songs, food, and drink at the fire, crucial conversations, laughs, and a few unforeseen betrayals. Tragedies hit hard. Occasionally there are glorious victories, and—hopefully not too often—crushing defeats.

Entrusting ourselves to God doesn't mean life's adventure fades into days of ease and comfort. Life doesn't always "go better with God." It's more often like my gray-haired pastor used to say with a grin, "Cheer up, saints! It's gonna get worse!" A quick glance through the life of Jesus in the Gospels and the lives of the apostles will show the truth in his humor. Some days we'll feel tired, down, and even wrecked. Paul lived this in the extreme: "But we have this treasure in earthen vessels, that the excellency of the power may be of God, and not of us. We are troubled on every side, yet not distressed; we are perplexed, but not in despair; persecuted, but not forsaken; cast down, but not destroyed; always bearing about in the body the dying of the Lord Jesus, that the life also of Jesus might be made manifest in our body" (2 Cor. 4:7–10 KJV).

. A life lived with God, a life of *knowing* God, of recognizing His life inside us, doesn't take away all of life's difficulties; rather, it gives us a solid ground for courage in life's adventure. We know He goes before and behind us, to the right and to the left, above and below. We know He's inside us.

We also know He's fully capable of scaring the enemy of our souls to make him cut and run. But in looking at the life of Jesus, it seems God allows situations in which we must trust Him more and more deeply, and in which we're pushed to look past the surface of circumstances to the heart of the matter—God's heart in the matter. God didn't scare off Goliath for David. David had to run at him with a sling and a stone. God didn't scare off the tempter for Jesus; Jesus had to hit him between the eyes with the spoken Word of God. And God didn't take Jesus off the cross; He had to go through death to gain resurrection for us all.

To walk in abiding dependence is to walk in the same dangerous world everyone else travels, but in relying on God we carry tools, weapons, and armor for protection, for advancement, and especially to protect those who are unprotected—we have gear many don't possess. We know we're protected, in an ultimate sense, from any real (i.e., eternal) harm.

God teaches us to know our enemy. He reveals valuable insight into his movements, motives, and covert ways, and He gives guidance as to what to do about it.

Sometimes we'll make mistakes. We'll forget to listen to God, and we'll push right past that inner feeling of "I shouldn't say this" or "I shouldn't do this," and there will be consequences. But we're to get back up as soon as possible, and turn, *metanoia*, to God, away from the sin. We take His forgiveness and get walking again. Then we make amends to the offended and face our consequences with guts.

We learn to crawl before we walk and walk before we run. Practicing dependence is, well, *practice*. And we get better with focused practice.

"I have told you these things so that in me you may have peace. In the world you have trouble and suffering, but take courage—I have conquered the world" (John 16:33 NET).

Acknowledgments

This devotional weaves together threads from many phases of my life, and there are quite a few people to thank for my continuing spiritual journey. First, to my wife, Sandra, for your consistent love and our decades of fun, growth, and God-conversations together, and for encouragement and suggestions for the book. Our son, Ethan, and daughter, Erica—you both put a lot of light in my heart, and I've learned so much about God by being your dad.

Eric Uglum, for being a wiser older brother to me for decades, and to Stacey.

Doris, Eric, Roddy, and Stephanie Uglum.

George and Janice Maxwell for trusting God and being the best in-laws.

My dad and stepmom, Chuck and Val Block, for love, a solid home base as a teen and young adult, and a good start in life. My mom, Joyce Block, for a life of love and encouragement. Gary Block for befriending the fourteen-year-old me and giving me a settled sense that life is good, and Lindsey Block. Dottie and

Larry Howell, and George and Georgia Block, for truly caring about my well-being.

Alison Krauss, Barry Bales, Dan Tyminski, and Jerry Douglas. Our journey has been beyond anything I could have dreamed up, and I'm so grateful for all of you.

Sylvia and Scott Pearce for your faithful love, wisdom, mentoring, and giving me freedom to be myself.

Rebecca Reynolds for always being a great friend.

Buddy Greene, Jeff Taylor, Kenny Thacker, and Clay Hess for music, God-talk, and general hilarity.

Andrew Peterson, Pete Peterson, and the amazing community of the Rabbit Room.

Craig Snyder for advice on some of the Greek words and your encouragement.

Dudley Hall, Scotty Smith, Steve Berger, Michael Wells, Gene Scott, Chuck and Nancy Missler.

To all my sisters, brothers, and cousins. All of you played big roles in my early life, and I'm grateful for every one of you.

Trillia Newbell and Mackenzie Conway at Moody Publishers for your encouragement, honesty, and hard work.

Andrew Osenga, thanks so much for suggesting me to Trillia as a Moody author.

Notes

Day 1: Life and Breath

1. "Lexicon: Strong's G4151 *pneuma*," Blue Letter Bible, accessed May 2, 2022, https://www.blueletterbible.org/lexicon/g4151/kjv/tr/0-1/.

2. C. S. Lewis, *Mere Christianity* (New York: HarperCollins, 2001), 198.

3. George MacDonald, *Diary of an Old Soul* (Minneapolis: Augsburg Fortress Press, 1994), 55.

Day 2: Jesus, the Son of God

Epigraph: George MacDonald, "Robert Falconer," in *The Complete Works of George MacDonald* (n.p.: Musaicum Books, 2017).

1. John 14:6; Revelation 21:6; Hebrews 12:2.

2. Dorothy Sayers, *Letters to a Diminished Church* (Nashville: W Publishing Group, 2004), 2.

Day 3: Jesus, the Son of Man

1. "Lexicon: Strong's G2296 *thaumazō*," Blue Letter Bible, accessed May 2, 2022, https://www.blueletterbible.org/lexicon/g2296/kjv/tr/0-1/.

2. Matthew 8:27; Mark 6:6; 15:44; Luke 11:38.

Day 4: Jesus, the Tempted Son of Man

1. "Lexicon: Strong's G5015 *tarassō*," Blue Letter Bible, accessed May 2, 2022, https://www.blueletterbible.org/lexicon/g5015/kjv/tr/0-1/.

Day 5: Jesus, Our Compassionate High Priest

1. C. S. Lewis, *Mere Christianity* (New York: HarperCollins, 2001), 225–26.

2. "Lexicon: Strong's G747 *archēgos*," Blue Letter Bible, accessed May 2, 2022, https://www.blueletterbible.org/lexicon/g747/kjv/tr/0-1/.

Day 6: Jesus, Man of Courage

Epigraph: C. S. Lewis, *The Screwtape Letters* (New York: HarperCollins, 2001), 161.

Day 8: The Abiding Dependence of Jesus

Epigraph: A. B. Simpson, *Christ in You: The Christ-Life and the Self-Life* (Chicago: Moody Publishers, 2014), 35.

Day 9: Jesus the Reconciler

1. C. S. Lewis, *The Great Divorce* (New York: The Macmillan Company, 1946), 26.

Day 10: What the Humanity of Jesus Means for Us

1. C. S. Lewis, *Mere Christianity* (New York: HarperCollins, 2001), 50.

2. C. S. Lewis, *The Screwtape Letters* (New York: HarperCollins, 2001), 161.

Day 11: The Serpent on the Pole

1. George MacDonald, *Unspoken Sermons Series I, II, III* (Whitehorn, CA: Johannesen Publishing, 1999), 391.

Day 12: What the Cross Means for Us

1. Major Ian Thomas, *The Indwelling Life of Christ* (Colorado Springs: Multnomah Books, 2006), 55.

2. See Romans 6:3–4; 7:4; 8:2.

Day 14: Grace and Law

1. Major Ian Thomas, "Christ in You, the Hope of Glory," video, https://www.thebodyofchrist.us/sermon/11263/.

Day 15: Belief Often Determines Experience

1. Major Ian Thomas, *The Indwelling Life of Christ* (Colorado Springs: Multnomah Books, 2006), 54.

Day 16: In Christ

1. 1 Corinthians 1:2; 15:19; 2 Corinthians 2:14; 1 Corinthians 1:30.

Day 17: Belief and Faith

1. "Lexicon: Strong's G4100 *pisteuō*," Blue Letter Bible, accessed May 2, 2022, https://www.blueletterbible.org/lexicon/g4100/kjv/tr/0-1/.

Day 18: Be Weak

1. "Lexicon: Strong's G2872 *kopiaō*," Blue Letter Bible, accessed May 2, 2022, https://www.blueletterbible.org/lexicon/g2872/kjv/tr/0-1/.

Day 19: Light and Seeing

1. See Matthew 5:14–15; Luke 1:79; 8:17.
2. C. S. Lewis, *Mere Christianity* (New York: HarperCollins, 2001), 226.
3. George MacDonald, *Alec Forbes of Howglen* (Whitehorn, CA: Johannesen Publishing, 2003), 315.

Day 20: *Metanoia*: Children of Mercy

1. "Lexicon: Strong's G3341 *metanoia*," Blue Letter Bible, accessed May 2, 2022, https://www.blueletterbible.org/lexicon/g3341/kjv/tr/0-1/.
2. "Lexicon: Strong's H7725 *šûb*," Blue Letter Bible, accessed May 2, 2022, https://www.blueletterbible.org/lexicon/h7725/kjv/wlc/0-1/.
3. Amy Carmichael, *Candles in the Dark: Letters of Hope and Encouragement* (Fort Washington, PA: CLC Publications, 2012), 19.

Day 21: Sunlight on the Dust: Sons and Daughters of God

1. C. S. Lewis, *The Screwtape Letters* (New York: HarperCollins, 2001), 19.

Day 22: A Father Addresses His Sons

1. George MacDonald, *The Hope of the Gospel* (Whitehorn, CA: Johannesen Publishing, 2000), 110–11.

Day 23: Named and Blessed

1. George MacDonald, *Sir Gibbie* (Whitehorn, CA: Johannesen Publishing, 1992), 161.

Day 24: God the Giver

1. "Lexicon: Strong's G26 *agapē*," Blue Letter Bible, accessed May 2, 2022, blueletterbible.org/lexicon/g26/kjv/tr/0-1/.

Day 25: Believing Is Seeing

1. "Lexicon: Strong's H2620 *hāsâ*," Blue Letter Bible, accessed May 2, 2022, https://www.blueletterbible.org/lexicon/h2620/kjv/wlc/0-1/.

Day 27: Children of the Father

1. George MacDonald, *Unspoken Sermons Series I, II, III* (Whitehorn, CA: Johannesen Publishing, 1999), 589.

2. Ibid., 479.

Day 28: Fear Not

1. "Lexicon: Strong's G2293 *tharseō*," Blue Letter Bible, accessed May 2, 2022, https://www.blueletterbible.org/lexicon/g2293/kjv/tr/0-1/.

Day 30: Electricity

1. "Lexicon: Strong's G5485 *charis*," Blue Letter Bible, accessed May 2, 2022, https://www.blueletterbible.org/lexicon/g5485/kjv/tr/0-1/.

2. *Thayer's Greek Lexicon*, Strong's NT G5485, accessed May 2, 2022, https://biblehub.com/greek/5485.htm.

Day 31: Filled Full

1. "Lexicon: Strong's G4138 *plērōma*," Blue Letter Bible, accessed May 2, 2022, https://www.blueletterbible.org/lexicon/g4138/kjv/tr/0-1/.

2. "Lexicon: Strong's G4137 *plēroō*," Blue Letter Bible, accessed May 2, 2022, https://www.blueletterbible.org/lexicon/g4137/kjv/tr/0-1/.

3. "Lexicon: Strong's G4053 *perissos*," Blue Letter Bible, accessed May 2, 2022, https://www.blueletterbible.org/lexicon/g4053/kjv/tr/0-1/.

Day 32: Dearly Loved

1. C. S. Lewis, *The Silver Chair* (New York: HarperCollins, 1998), 432.

Day 35: Fire

1. Mrs. Charles E. Cowman, "December 18," in *Springs in the Valley* (Grand Rapids, MI: Zondervan, 2010).

2. George MacDonald, *Unspoken Sermons Series I, II, III* (Whitehorn, CA: Johannesen Publishing, 1999), 24.

3. Ibid.,18–19.

Day 36: Courage to Leap

1. C. S. Lewis, *Prince Caspian* (New York: HarperCollins, 1998), 260–62.

Day 40: Peter, the Rock

1. "Lexicon: Strong's G4074 *petros*," Blue Letter Bible, accessed May 2, 2022, https://www.blueletterbible.org/lexicon/g4074/kjv/tr/0-1/.

"The best association for the word sacramental is Jesus. Yes, Jesus—the wonderful grace of Jesus; the glory of Jesus, His face shining like the sun; the life of Jesus, overflowing like a thousand geysers into our world."

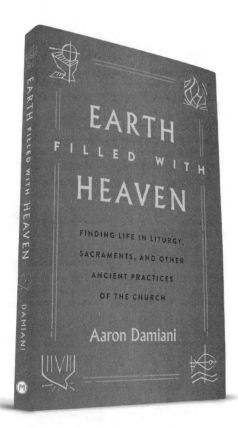

MOODY
Publishers®

From the Word to Life®

Christians from a low-church background do not have to be afraid of liturgy and sacraments. On the contrary, these ancient ways of engaging with Scripture and faith help us see the beauty and taste the grace of heaven through the incarnation of Jesus. *Earth Filled with Heaven* is an evangelical introduction to the theological framework and habits of the sacramental life.

978-0-8024-2536-2 I also available as eBook and audiobook

"What comes into our minds when we think about God is the most important thing about us."
—A. W. Tozer

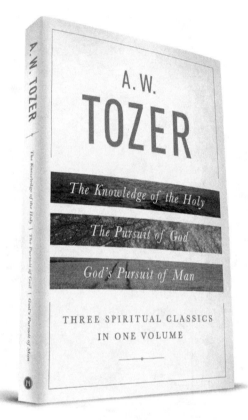

MOODY
Publishers®

*From the Word **to Life**®*

Considered to be Tozer's greatest works, *The Knowledge of the Holy*, *The Pursuit of God*, and *God's Pursuit of Man* are now available in a single volume. Discover a God of breathtaking majesty and world-changing love, and find yourself worshiping through every page.

978-0-8024-1861-6

"Let the morning bring me word of your unfailing love, for I have put my trust in you. Show me the way I should go, for to you I entrust my life."

—Psalm 143:8 (NIV)

MOODY Publishers®

From the Word to Life®

Many of these 365 devotional readings come from sermons Tozer preached close to his death in 1963, marking them with a deep concern for spiritual intimacy and true worship. He urges you to pursue God, confess sin, pray fervently, and seek the Spirit. Let this book be a garnish in your feast of God's Word.

978-1-60066-794-7 | also available as eBook and audiobook